SMITH'S ACCOUNT OF TAKING THE "GOLDEN BIBLE" FROM MORMON HILL.

ORIGIN, RISE, AND PROGRESS

OF

MORMONISM.

BIOGRAPHY OF ITS FOUNDERS AND HISTORY OF ITS CHURCH.

PERSONAL REMEMBRANCES AND HISTORICAL COLLECTIONS HITHERTO UNWRITTEN.

BY POMEROY TUCKER,

PALMYRA, N. Y.

NEW YORK:

D. APPLETON AND COMPANY,

443 & 445 BROADWAY.

1867.

PREFACE.

Mormonism, in its progress and maturity, has attained a conspicuous page in the annals of our century. Yet a full account of the remarkable sect, beginning with its origin and rise, and circumstantially disclosing the earlier designs and delusions of its founders, has hitherto remained unwritten. The facts and reminiscences contained in this volume, based upon the author's personal knowledge and information, are produced to fill the blank and supply the omitted chapters in Mormon history.

Chronologically tracing the Church of Latter-Day Saints, from its singularly humble starting-point, through a wonderfully successful career of domination by crafty leaders over blind infatuation, to its assumed dignity of a newly-revealed gospel dispensation, with its extraordinary hierarchal powers and pretensions, this truthful narrative is necessary to the completion of the history from the foundation of the institution. Events and incidents, which at their occurrence were viewed by enlightened minds as too insignificant for serious thought, are now rescued from oblivion for record and preservation, as important illustrations of the groundwork of a stupendous imposture attaining an extended influence and world-wide notoriety.

In claiming for the statements herein set forth the character of fairness and authenticity, it is perhaps appropriate to add in this connection, that the locality of the malversations resulting in the Mormon scheme, is the author's birthplace; that he was well acquainted with "Joe Smith," the first Mormon prophet, and with his father and all the Smith family, since their removal to Palmyra from Vermont in 1816, and during their continuance there and in the adjoining town of Manchester; that he was equally acquainted with Martin Harris and Oliver Cowdery, and with most of the earlier followers of Smith, either as money-diggers or Mormons; that he established at Palmyra, in 1823, and was for many years editor and proprietor of the *Wayne Sentinel*, and was editorially connected with that paper at the printing by its press of the original edition of the "Book of Mormon" in 1830; that in the progress of the work he performed much of the reading of the proof-sheets, comparing the same with the manuscript copies, and in the mean time had frequent and familiar interviews with the pioneer Mormons, Smith, Cowdery, and Harris; that he was present at the repeated consultations and negotiations between these men and Mr. Grandin in relation to the printing of the book, and united with the latter in the friendly admonitions vainly seeking to divert Harris from his persistent fanaticism in that losing speculation.

For corroboratory references, the author is permitted to name Messrs. Joseph Capron, Russell Stoddard, Barton Stafford, and Russell M. Rush, of Manchester, N. Y.; and Messrs. George Beckwith, George W. Cuyler, Richard S. Williams, Willard Chase, John H. Gilbert, and Joseph C. Lovett, of Palmyra; who, with himself (except the last two named), were contemporaries and neighbors of Smith and his family for the whole period of their residence in this locality, and all of whom were familiar with their character and pursuits, and with their money-digging reputation and fabulous "Golden Bible" discovery.

The data for the later chapters of this Mormon history, have been obtained from private correspondence, personal communications, official records, and various published works.

POMEROY TUCKER.

PALMYRA, N. Y., *May*, 1867.

LETTER OF THURLOW WEED.

MR. WEED resided at Rochester, near the scene of Smith's delusive practices, at the time of the inception and development of the Mormon invention, and knew either personally or by common fame the chief impostor and his followers. The letter below will explain itself:

NEW YORK, *June* 1, 1867.

DEAR SIR: I have been so constantly occupied, that I really did not get time to say how much I was interested in your history of Mormonism. I have long hoped that some person with personal knowledge of the origin of this great delusion—who saw it as I did, when it was "no bigger than a man's hand," and who has the courage and capacity to tell the whole truth, would undertake the task. I read enough of your manuscript to be confident that you have discharged this duty faithfully. The character you have given "Joe Smith," his family and associates, corresponds with what I have often heard from the old citizens of Palmyra. Such a work is wanted, and no one but a writer personally and familiarly acquainted with the false prophet and his surroundings could have written it.

Truly yours,

THURLOW WEED.

CONTENTS.

CHAPTER XVI.

APPENDIX.

MORMONISM:

ITS ORIGIN, RISE, AND PROGRESS.

CHAPTER I.

Biography of Joseph Smith, Jr.—Early Life and Times of the Smith Family—Their Character and Employments.

JOSEPH SMITH, Jr., who in the subsequent pages appears in the character of the first Mormon prophet, and the putative founder of Mormonism and the Church of Latter Day Saints, was born in Sharon, Windsor County, Vt., December 13, 1805. He was the son of Joseph Smith, Sr., who, with his wife Lucy and their family, removed from Royalton, Vt., to Palmyra, N. Y., in the summer of 1816. The family embraced nine children, Joseph, Jr., being the fourth in the order of their ages, viz.: Alvin, Hyrum (so spelled by his father), Sophronia, JOSEPH, Samuel H., William, Catherine, Carlos, and Lucy. These constituted the chief earthly possessions and responsibilities of Mr. and Mrs. Smith at the time of their emigration to Western New York.

At Palmyra, Mr. Smith, Sr., opened a "cake and beer shop," as described by his signboard, doing business on a small scale, by the profits of which, added to the earnings of an occasional day's work on hire by himself and his elder sons, for the village and farming people, he was understood to secure a scanty but honest living for himself and family. These hired days' works were divided among the various common labor jobs that offered from time to time, such as gardening, harvesting, well-digging, etc.

Mr. Smith's shop merchandise, consisting of gingerbread, pies, boiled eggs, root-beer, and other like notions of traffic, soon became popular with the juvenile people of the town and country, commanding brisk sales, especially on Fourth of July anniversaries, and on military training days, as these prevailed at that period. Peddling was done in the streets on those occasions by the facility of a rude handcart of the proprietor's own construction.

Mr. Smith and his household continued their residence in Palmyra village, living in the manner described, for some two and a half years. In 1818 they settled upon a nearly wild or unimproved piece of land, mostly covered with standing timber, situate about two miles south of Palmyra, being on the north border of the town of Manchester, Ontario County.

The title of this landed property was vested in non-resident minor heirs; and the premises being uncared for by any local agent or attorney, the Smiths took possession of it by the rights of "squatter sovereignty." They thus remained unmolested in its possession for some twelve years, occupying as their dwelling-place, in the first instance, a small, one-story, smoky log-house, which they had built prior to removing there. This house was divided into two rooms, on the ground-floor, and had a low garret, in two apartments. A bedroom wing, built of sawed slabs, was afterward added.

Subsequently this property was purchased by Mr. Smith on contract, a small payment thereon being made by him to bind the bargain; and in this way his occupancy of the premises was prolonged until after the blooming of the Mormon scheme in 1829.

But little improvement was made upon this land by the Smith family in the way of clearing, fencing, or tillage. Their farm-work was done in a slovenly, half-way, profitless manner. Shortly before quitting the premises they erected a small frame-house thereon, partly enclosed, and never finished by them, in which they lived for the remainder of their time there, using their original log hut for a barn. This property, finally vacated by the Smiths in 1831, is now included in the well-organized farm of Mr. Seth T. Chapman, on Stafford Street, running south from Palmyra.

The chief application of the useful industry of the Smiths during their residence upon this farm-lot, was in the chopping and retailing of cord-wood, the raising and bartering of small crops of agricultural products and garden vegetables, the manufacture and sale of black-ash baskets and birch brooms, the making of maple sugar and molasses in the season for that work, and in the continued business of peddling cake and beer in the village on days of public doings. It was as a clerk in this last-mentioned line of trade that the rising Joseph (the prophet to be) learned his first lessons in commercial and monetary science. And in this connection it may not be out of place to state, in the way of illustration in respect to the beginning of human greatness on his part—though the mention of the fact is by no means creditable to the memory of the mischievous parties implicated—that the boys of those by-gone times used to delight in obtaining the valuable goods intrusted to Joseph's clerkship, in exchange for worthless pewter imitation two-shilling pieces.

The larger proportion of the time of the Smiths, however, was spent in hunting and fishing, trapping muskrats ("mushrats" was the word they used), digging out woodchucks from their holes, and idly lounging around the stores and shops in the village. Joseph generally took the leading direction of the rural enterprises mentioned, instead of going to school like other boys—though he was seldom known personally to participate in the practical *work* involved in these or any other pursuits. Existing as they did from year to year in this thriftless manner, with seemingly inadequate visible means or habits of profitable industry for their respectable livelihood, it is not at all to be wondered at that the suspicions of some good people in the community were apt to be turned toward them, especially in view of the frequently occurring nocturnal depredations and thefts in the neighborhood. On these accounts the inhabitants came to observe more than their former vigilance in the care of their sheepfolds, hencoops, smoke-houses, pork-barrels, and the like domestic interests; though it is but common fairness to accompany this fact by the statement, that it is not within the remembrance of the writer, who in this designedly impartial narrative would "nothing extenuate nor aught set down in malice," if the popular inferences in this matter were ever sustained by judicial investigation.

It is appropriate to remark, however, that the truth of history, no less than proper deference to the recollections of many living witnesses in Palmyra and its vicinity, demand that these reminiscences should be given, intimately blended as they are with the purpose in hand, to present before the public a candid and authentic account of the origin, rise, and progress of Mormonism, from its first foundation.

At this period in the life and career of Joseph Smith, Jr., or "Joe Smith," as he was universally named, and the Smith family, they were popularly regarded as an illiterate, whiskey-drinking, shiftless, irreligious race of people—the first named, the chief subject of this biography, being unanimously voted the laziest and most worthless of the generation. From the age of twelve to twenty years he is distinctly remembered as a dull-eyed, flaxen-haired, prevaricating boy—noted only for his indolent and vagabondish character, and his habits of exaggeration and untruthfulness. Taciturnity was among his characteristic idiosyncrasies, and he seldom spoke to any one outside of his intimate associates, except when first addressed by another; and then, by reason of his extravagancies of statement, his word was received with the least confidence by those who knew him best. He could utter the most palpable exaggeration or marvellous absurdity with the utmost apparent gravity. He nevertheless evidenced the rapid development of a thinking, plodding, evil-brewing mental composition—largely given to inventions of low cunning, schemes of mischief and deception, and false and mysterious pretensions. In his moral phrenology the professor might have marked the organ of secretiveness as very large, and that of conscientiousness "omitted." He was, however, proverbially good-natured, very rarely if ever indulging in any combative spirit toward any one, whatever might be the provocation, and yet was never known to laugh. Albeit, he seemed to be the pride of his indulgent father, who has been heard to boast of him as the "*genus* of the family," quoting his own expression.

Joseph, moreover, as he grew in years, had learned to read comprehensively, in which qualification he was far in advance of his elder brother, and even of his father; and this talent was assiduously devoted, as he quitted or modified his idle habits, to the perusal of works of fiction and records of criminality, such for instance as would be classed with the "dime novels" of the present day. The stories of Stephen Burroughs and Captain Kidd, and the like, presented the highest charms for his expanding mental perceptions. As he further advanced in reading and knowledge, he assumed a spiritual or religious turn of mind, and frequently perused the Bible, becoming quite familiar with portions thereof, both of the Old and New Testaments; selected texts from which he quoted and discussed with great assurance when in the presence of his superstitious acquaintances. The Prophecies and Revelations were his special forte. His interpretations of scriptural passages were always original and unique, and his deductions and conclusions often disgustingly blasphemous, according to the common apprehensions of Christian people.

Protracted revival meetings were customary in

some of the churches, and Smith frequented those of different denominations, sometimes professing to participate in their devotional exercises. At one time he joined the probationary class of the Methodist church in Palmyra, and made some active demonstrations of engagedness, though his assumed convictions were insufficiently grounded or abiding to carry him along to the saving point of conversion, and he soon withdrew from the class. The final conclusion announced by him was, that all sectarianism was fallacious, all the churches on a false foundation, and the Bible a fable.

In unbelief, theory and practice, the Smith family, all as one, so far as they held any definable position upon the subject of religion—basing this conclusion upon all the early avowals and other evidences remembered, as well as upon the subsequent developments extant—were unqualified atheists. Can their mockeries of Christianity, their persistent blasphemies, be accounted for upon any other hypothesis?

CHAPTER II.

Smith's Money-Digging—How it began—Magic Stone—A Vision—Wonderful Discoveries—Fanatics and Dupes.

In September, 1819, a curious stone was found in the digging of a well upon the premises of Mr. Clark Chase, near Palmyra. This stone attracted particular notice on account of its peculiar shape, resembling that of a child's foot. It was of a whitish, glassy appearance, though opaque, resembling quartz. Joseph Smith, Sr., and his elder sons Alvin and Hyrum, did the chief labor of this well-digging, and Joseph, Jr., who had been a frequenter in the progress of the work, as an idle looker-on and lounger, manifested a special fancy for this geological curiosity; and he carried it home with him, though this act of plunder was against the strenuous protestations of Mr. Chase's children, who claimed to be its rightful owners.

Joseph kept this stone, and ever afterward refused its restoration to the claimants. Very soon the pretension transpired that he could see wonderful things by its aid. This idea was rapidly enlarged upon from day to day, and in a short time his spiritual endowment was so developed that he asserted the gift and power (with the stone at his eyes) of revealing both things existing and things to come.

For a length of time this clairvoyant manifestation was sought to be turned to selfish advantage, in the way of fortune-telling, and in the pretended discovery by the medium of the seer-stone of lost or stolen property. But the realizations from these sources were insufficient to encourage a long continuance of the experiments, though some small amounts were obtained by them; and a very worthy citizen now living in Palmyra actually paid seventy-five cents in money for being sent some three miles on a fool's errand in pursuit of a stolen roll of cloth. It is presumed to be needless to add, that no genuine discoveries of stolen property were made in this manner, and that the entire proceeds derived from the speculation went into Joe's pocket.

The most glittering sights revealed to the mortal vision of the young impostor in the manner stated, were hidden treasures of great value, including enormous deposits of gold and silver sealed in earthen pots or iron chests, and buried in the earth in the immediate vicinity of the place where he stood. These discoveries finally became too dazzling for his eyes in daylight, and he had to shade his vision by looking at the stone in his hat! Of course but few persons were sufficiently stolid to listen to these silly pretensions, for they were only of a piece with Joe's habitual extravagances of assertion. Yet he may have had believers.

Persisting in this claim to the gift of spiritual discernment, Smith very soon succeeded in his experiment upon the credulity of a selected audience of ignorant and superstitious persons, to an extent which it is presumed he could not himself have anticipated at the outset of the trial. He followed up this advantage, and by its means, in the spring of 1820, raised some small contributions from the people in the vicinity, to defray the expense of digging for the buried money, the precise hiding-place of which he had discovered by the aid of the stone in his hat. At an appointed time, being at a dead hour of night, his dupes and employed laborers repaired with lanterns to the revealed locality of the treasure, which was upon the then forest hill, a short distance from his father's house; and after some preparatory mystic ceremonies, the work of digging began at his signal. Silence, as the condition of success, had been enjoined upon the chosen few present, who were to be sharers in the expected prize. The excavating process was continued for some two hours, without a word being spoken—the magician meanwhile indicating, by some sort of a wand in his hand, the exact spot where the spade was to be crowded into the earth—when, just at the moment the money-box was within the seer's grasp, one of the party, being "tempted by the devil," *spoke!* The enchantment was broken, and the treasure vanished! Such was Joe's explanation, and, ridiculous as was the idea, it was apparently satisfactory to his dupes.

This was the inauguration of the impostor's money-digging performances; and the description given of this first trial and of its results is as near exactitude as can at this time be recollected from his own accounts. Several of the individuals participating in this and subsequent diggings, and many others well remembering the stories of the time, are yet living witnesses of these follies, and can make suitable corrections if the particulars as stated are not substantially according to the facts.

The imposture was renewed and repeated at frequent intervals from 1820 to 1827, various localities being the scenes of these delusive searches for money, as pointed out by the revelations of the magic stone. And these tricks of young Smith were not too absurd for the credence of his fanatical followers. He was sufficiently artful and persevering to preserve his spell-holding power over their minds, and keep up his deceptions for the length of time before stated. It certainly evidences extraordinary talent or subtlety, that for so long a period he could maintain the potency of his art over numbers of beings in the form of manhood, acknowledging their faith in his supernatural powers. He continued to use this advantage in the progress of his experiments to raise from them and others contributions in money and various articles of value, amounting to a considerable aggregate sum, being enough to pay the digging expenses (whiskey and labor), and also in this way securing a handsome surplus, which went in part toward necessary domestic supplies for the Smith family.

In some instances individuals were impelled, in their donations in this business, by the motive of ridding themselves of Smith's importunities, while others advanced the idea that there "might be something in it," as they explained in reply to the unfavorable suggestions of reflecting friends. One respectable and forehanded citizen, now living in Manchester, confesses to having patronized Smith's perseverance on this idea, and says he once handed him a silver dollar, partly in that view and partly to "get rid of the fellow." Smith's father and elder brothers generally participated in the manual labors of these diggings, and their example seemed to revive confidence in the sometimes wavering victims of the imposture, and also to bring others to their aid.

The subsequent operations on this head were conducted substantially in the mode and manner of the first performance, as described, with slight variations in the incantations, and always with the same result—Smith "almost" getting hold of the money-chest, but finally losing it by the coincident breaking of the "spell" through some unforeseen satanic interposition. By this cause the money would *vanish* just at the instant of its coming within the necromancer's mortal grasp!

A single instance of Smith's style of conducting these money-diggings will suffice for the whole series, and also serve to illustrate his low cunning, and show the strange infatuation of the persons who yielded to his unprincipled designs. Assuming his accustomed air of mystery on one of the occasions, and pretending to see by his miraculous stone exactly where the sought-for chest of money had lodged in its subterranean transits, Smith gave out the revelation that a "black sheep" would be required as a sacrificial offering upon the enchanted ground before entering upon the work of exhumation. He knew that his kind-hearted neighbor, William Stafford,* who was a listener to his plausible story—a respectable farmer in comfortable worldly circumstances—possessed a fine, fat, black wether, intended for division between his family use and the village market, and Smith knew, moreover, that fresh meat was a rarity at his father's home

* Mr. Stafford, beginning in early life, had been for many years a sailor, and was largely prone to the vagaries and superstitions peculiar to his class. He was thus an easy victim.

where he lived. The scheme succeeded completely. It was arranged that Mr. Stafford should invest the wether as his stock in the speculation, the avails of which were to be equitably shared among the company engaging in it. At the approach of the appointed hour at night, the digging fraternity, with lanterns, and the fattened sheep for the sacrifice, were conducted by Smith to the place where the treasure was to be obtained. There Smith described a circle upon the ground around the buried chest, where the blood of the animal was to be shed as the necessary condition of his power to secure the glittering gold. As usual, not a word was to be spoken during the ceremony, nor until after the prize was brought forth. All things being thus in readiness, the throat of the sheep was cut by one of the party according to previous instructions, the poor animal made to pour its own blood around the circle, and the excavation entered upon in a vigorous and solemn manner. In this case the digging was continued for about three hours, when the "devil" again frustrated the plan exactly in the same way as on the repeated trials before! In the mean time, the elder Smith, aided by one of the junior sons, had withdrawn the sacrificial carcass and reduced its flesh to mutton for his family use.

Such is a true account, so far as it goes, of the long-continued and astonishingly successful career of vice and deception led by Joseph Smith, Jr., which is believed to be ample in detail for the object of this publication. These delusions, persevered in and improved upon from time to time, culminated in 1827 by the great imposture of the pretended finding of the "ancient metallic plates resembling gold," afterward translated into the "Golden Bible" or Book of Mormon, as will be explained in subsequent pages.

Numerous traces of the excavations left by Smith are yet remaining as evidences of his impostures and the folly of his dupes, though most of them have become obliterated by the clearing off and tilling of the lands where they were made.

It is an interesting illustrative fact to be noticed in the history of Mormonism, as will hereafter be seen, that the origin of that extraordinary politico-religious institution is traceable to the insignificant little stone found in the digging of Mr. Chase's well in 1819. Such was the acorn of the Mormon oak.

CHAPTER III.

Mysterious Stranger—Smith has a remarkable Vision—He assumes to be a Prophet—Finding of the Golden Bible and Urim and Thummim—Frightful Phenomenon—Translations—How received by the Public.

THE fame of Smith's money-digging performances had been sounded far and near. The newspapers had heralded and ridiculed them. The pit-hole memorials of his treasure explorations were numerous in the surrounding fields and woodlands, attracting the inspection of the curious, and the wonder of the superstitious. The outgivings of "spiritual demonstrations," in various forms and in different parts of the country, had perhaps contributed in preparing the fanatical mind for some extraordinary revelation. Notwithstanding the failure of seven or eight years' continued efforts for the attainment of the promised wealth from its hidden earthy deposit, yet "the fools were not all dead," and the time might have seemed opportune for the prediction of some marvellous discovery, and for the great "religious" event that was to follow in the career of Joe Smith!

This review comes down to the summer of 1827. A mysterious stranger now appears at Smith's residence, and holds private interviews with the far-famed money-digger. For a considerable length of time no intimation of the name or purpose of this personage transpired to the public, nor even to Smith's nearest neighbors. It was observed by some of them that his visits were frequently repeated. The sequel of these private interviews between the stranger and the money-digger will sufficiently appear hereafter.

About this time Smith had a remarkable vision. He pretended that, while engaged in secret prayer, alone in the wilderness, an "angel of the Lord" appeared to him, with the glad tidings that "all his sins had been forgiven," and proclaiming further that "all the religious denominations were believing in false doctrines, and consequently that none of them were accepted of God as of His Church and Kingdom;" also that he had received a "promise that the true doctrine and the fulness of the gospel should at some future time be revealed to him. Following this, soon came another angel, (or possibly the same one,) revealing to him that he was himself to be "the favored instrument of the new revelation;" "that the American Indians were a remnant of the Israelites, who, after coming to this country, had their prophets and inspired writings; that such of their writings as had not been destroyed were safely deposited in a certain place made known to him, and to him only; that they contained revelations in regard to the last days, and that, if he remained faithful, he would be the chosen prophet to translate them to the world."

In the fall of the same year Smith had yet a more miraculous and astonishing vision than any preceding one. He now arrogated to himself, by authority of "the spirit of revelation," and in accordance with the previous "promises" made to him, a far higher sphere in the scale of human existence, assuming to possess the gift and power of "prophet, seer, and revelator." On this assumption he announced to his family friends and the bigoted persons who had adhered to his supernaturalism, that he was "commanded," upon a secretly fixed day and hour, to go alone to a certain spot revealed to him by the angel, and there take out of the earth a metallic book of great antiquity in its origin, and of immortal importance in its consequences to the world, which was a record, in mystic letters or characters, of the long-lost tribes of Israel before spoken of, who had primarily inhabited this continent, and which no human being besides himself could see and live; and the power to translate which to the nations of the earth was also given to him only, as the chosen servant of God! This was substantially, if not literally, the pretension of Smith, as related by himself, and repeatedly quoted by his credulous friends at the time.

Much pains were taken by the Smith family and the prophet's money-digging disciples to give wide circulation to the wonderful revelation, and in great gravity to predict its marvellous fulfilment. It is unknown, however, if the momentous announcement produced any sensation in the community, though it is fair to presume that the victims of Smith's former deceptive practices regarded it with some seriousness.

Accordingly, when the appointed hour came, the prophet, assuming his practised air of mystery, took in hand his money-digging spade and a large napkin, and went off in silence and alone in the solitude of the forest, and after an absence of some three hours, returned, apparently with his sacred charge concealed within the folds of the napkin. Reminding the family of the original "command" as revealed to him, strict injunction of non-intervention and non-inspection was given to them, under the same terrible penalty as before denounced for its violation. Conflicting stories were afterward told in regard to the manner of keeping the book in concealment and safety, which are not worth repeating, further than to mention that the first place of secretion was said to be under a heavy hearthstone in the Smith family mansion.

Smith told a frightful story of the display of celestial pyrotechnics on the exposure to his view of the sacred book—the angel who had led him to the discovery again appearing as his guide and protector, and confronting ten thousand devils gathered there, with their menacing sulphureous flame and smoke, to deter him from his purpose! This story was repeated and magnified by the believers, and no doubt aided the experiment upon superstitious minds which eventuated so successfully.

Mr. Willard Chase, a carpenter and joiner, was called upon by Smith and requested to make a strong chest in which to keep the golden book under lock and key, in order to prevent the awful calamity that would follow against the person other than himself who should behold it with his natural eyes. He could not pay a shilling for the work, and therefore proposed to make Mr. Chase a sharer in the profits ultimately anticipated in some manner not definitely stated; but the proposition was rejected—the work was refused on the terms offered. It was understood, however, that the custodian of the precious treasure afterward in some way procured a chest for his purpose, which, with its sacred deposit, was kept in a dark garret of his father's house, where the translations were subsequently made, as will be explained. An anecdote touching this subject used to be related by William T. Hussey and Azel Vandruver. They were notorious wags, and were intimately acquainted with Smith. They called as his friends at his residence, and strongly importuned him for an inspection of the "golden book," offering to take upon themselves the risk of the death-penalty denounced. Of course, the request could not be complied with; but they were permitted to go to the chest with its owner, and see *where* the thing was, and observe its shape and size, concealed under a piece of thick canvas. Smith, with his accustomed solemnity of demeanor, positively persisting in his refusal to uncover it, Hussey became impetuous, and (suiting his action to his word) ejaculated, "Egad! I'll see the critter, live or die!" And stripping off the cover, a large tile-brick was exhibited. But Smith's fertile imagination was equal to the emergency. He claimed that his friends had been sold by a trick of his; and "treating" with the customary whiskey hospitalities, the affair ended in good-nature.

With the book was also found, or so pretended, a huge pair of spectacles in a perfect state of preservation, or the *Urim* and *Thummim*,* as afterward in-

* The best attainable definition of the very ancient Urim and Thummim is quite vague and indistinct. An accepted biblical lexicographer gives the meaning as "light and perfection," or the "shining and the perfect." The following is quoted from Butterworth's Concordance: "There are various conjectures about the Urim and Thummim, whether they were the stones in the high-priest's breast-plate, or something distinct from them; which it is not worth our while to inquire into, since God has left it a secret. It is evident that the Urim and Thummim were appointed to inquire of God by, on momentous occasions, and continued in use (as some think) only till the building of Solomon's Temple, and all conclude that this was never restored after its destruction."

terpreted, whereby the mystic record was to be translated and the wonderful dealings of God revealed to man, by the superhuman power of Joe Smith. This spectacle pretension, however, is believed to have been purely an after-thought, for it was not heard of outside of the Smith family for a considerable period subsequent to the first story. So in regard to Smith's after-averment, that he had received a revelation of the existence of the records in 1823, but was not permitted to touch or mention them until "the fulness of time" should come for the great event, this idea was also a secondary invention.

The marvellous metallic book and its accompaniment soon became a common topic of conversation, far and near; but the sacred treasure was not seen by mortal eyes, save those of the one anointed, until after the lapse of a year or longer time, when it was found expedient to have a new revelation, as Smith's bare word had utterly failed to gain a convert beyond his original circle of believers. By this amended revelation, the veritable existence of the book was certified to by eleven witnesses of Smith's selection. It was then heralded as the Golden Bible, or Book of Mormon,* and as the beginning of a new gospel dispensation. Wonderful stories and predictions fol-

* Philologically, "Mormon" is probably synonymous with *mormo*, which, according to Webster, signifies "bugbear—false terror." At least, this definition is sufficiently appropriate.

lowed in regard to the future "light" and destiny of the world, but these were for a time very crude and very conflicting, and therefore scarcely definable or worth repeating; and they had little attraction for public notice or curiosity. The reader will be content with the narration of these things as they ultimately took shape and system.

The spot from which the book is alleged to have been taken, is the yet partially visible pit where the money speculators had previously dug for another kind of treasure, which is upon the summit of what has ever since been known as "Mormon Hill," now owned by Mr. Anson Robinson, in the town of Manchester, New York.

This book of sacred records, after the dispersion of the first vague reports concerning it, was finally described by Smith and his echoes as consisting of metallic leaves or plates resembling gold, bound together in a volume by three rings running through one edge of them, the leaves opening like an ordinary paper book. The leaves were about the thickness of common tin. Each leaf or plate was filled on both sides with engravings of finely-drawn characters, which resembled Egyptian or other hieroglyphics. The Urim and Thummim, found with the records, were two transparent crystals set in the rims of a bow, in the form of spectacles of enormous size. This constituted the seer's instrument whereby the records were to be translated and the mysteries of hidden things revealed, and it was to supersede the further use of the magic stone. The entire sacred acquisition was delivered into the hands of the prophet by the heavenly messenger attending him, amid the awful surroundings already stated, after the former had thrown up a few spadefuls of earth in pursuance of the Lord's command. Such was Smith's ingenious story at the time, the characterization of which is left for the reader.

Translations and interpretations were now entered upon by the prophet, and manuscript specimens of these, with some of the literally transcribed characters, were shown to people, including ministers and other gentlemen of learning and influence. These translations purported to relate to the history of scattered tribes of the earth, chiefly "Nephites" and "Lamanites," who, after the confusion of tongues at the Tower of Babel, had been directed by the Lord across the sea to this then wilderness-land, where they mostly perished by wars among themselves, and by pestilence and famine, and from whose remnants sprang our North American Indians. They were an attempted imitation of the Scripture style of composition, containing some plagiarisms from the Bible, both the Old and New Testaments, drawing largely upon Isaiah and Jeremiah, and taking from Matthew nearly the whole of Christ's Sermon on the Mount, with some alterations. The manuscripts were in the handwriting of one Oliver Cowdery, which had been written down by him, as he and Smith declared, from the translations, word for word, as made by the latter with the aid of the mammoth spectacles or Urim and Thummim, and verbally announced by him from behind a blanket-screen drawn across a dark corner of a room at his residence—for at this time the original revelation, limiting to the prophet the right of seeing the sacred plates, had not yet been changed, and the view with the instrument used was even too brilliant for his own spiritualized eyes in the light! This was the story of the first series of translations, which was always persisted in by the few persons connected with the business at this early period of its progress. The single significance of this theory will doubtless be manifest, when the facts are stated in explanation, that Smith could not write in a legible hand, and hence an amanuensis or scribe was necessary. Cowdery had been a schoolmaster, and was the only man in the band who could make a copy for the printer.

The manifest purpose of exhibiting these manuscripts in the manner adopted, was to test the popular credulity in regard to their assumed divine character; and also to determine, by the responses that should be elicited, as to the practicability of carrying out a concocted design of printing the "new Bible." Among others, Mr. George Crane, of the adjoining town of Macedon, a Quaker of intelligence, property, and high respectability (now deceased), was called upon by Smith with several foolscap quires of these so-called translations, for his perusal and opinion, and also for his pecuniary aid to get the work through the press. The impious story, in all its extravagance and garniture, was related to him, to which he quietly listened to the end. And then came the answer of the honest old Quaker, which was such as would have been withering to the sensibility of an ordinary impostor—though Smith was unmoved by it, for his spirit of determination was never known to yield consentingly to any adverse human influence. Sternly rebuking Smith's pretensions, and denouncing them as in a high degree blasphemous and wicked, Mr. Crane kindly but earnestly admonished him, for his own good, to desist from his criminal pursuit, warning him that persistence therein would be certain to end in his death upon the gallows, or in some equally ignominious manner. How far this friendly warning was made prophetic, by the murderous catastrophe occurring fifteen years afterward, in Illinois, is a question respectfully submitted to the reader.

CHAPTER IV.

Budding of the Mormon Church—Proposed Printing of the Golden Bible—Martin Harris consults Professor Anthon and Others—Translations lost—Mysterious Stranger again.

Undaunted by any rebuffs, Prophet Smith persisted in his grand design, and, by the power of his expanding genius, secured a few devoted followers in this incipiency of his new revelation—proving that, in his case, "the prophet" was not wholly "without honor" even in his "own country." Here may be recognized the first budding of the Mormon organization, or "Church of Latter-Day Saints."

These pioneer Mormon disciples, so far as their names can now be recollected, were as follows, viz.: Oliver Cowdery, Samuel Lawrence, Martin Harris, Preserved Harris, Peter Ingersoll, Charles Ford, George Proper and his wife Dolly, of Palmyra; Ziba Peterson, and Calvin Stoddard and his wife Sophronia, of Macedon; Ezra Thayer, of Brighton; Luman Walters, of Pultneyville; Hiram Page, of

Fayette; David Whitmer, Jacob Whitmer, Christian Whitmer, John Whitmer, and Peter Whitmer, Jr., of Phelps; Simeon Nichols, of Farmington; William Stafford, Joshua Stafford, Gad Stafford, David Fish, Abram Fish, Robert Orr, King H. Quance, John Morgan, Orrin Rockwell and his wife Caroline, Widow Sally Risley, and all the remainder of the Smith family, of Manchester.

It is believed that this list embraces all the persons residing at or near the prime seat of the Mormon advent, who from first to last made a profession of belief either in the money-digging or golden bible finding pretensions of Joseph Smith, Jr.; and probably, indeed, not more than one-half of these can be said to have been genuine converts under the one head or the other. It is to be added in this connection, however, that a man of the name of Parley P. Pratt, of Lorain County, Ohio, who, on hearing of the new religion, after the Mormon book was printed (as he said in explanation of his movement), stopped off a canal-boat at Palmyra, and at Smith's residence embraced the Mormon faith, and joined the organization which had then been imperfectly inaugurated. He was a member of an association of anti-sectarians, mostly dissenters from different religious denominations, whose place of worship was at Mentor, Ohio. "Rev. Sidney Rigdon" was the regular minister of this congregation; though Pratt himself had done something in the way of preaching there and elsewhere, and was aspiring to still higher position in the clerical vocation. The latter, with his spiritual guide Rigdon, afterward went with the first emigrants to Kirtland, and, continuing his association with the new sect, immediately became a prominent and efficient co-worker in its priesthood, and was subsequently an important spoke in the Mormon hierarchy at Salt Lake.*

How many of the preceding list of pioneer "Latter-Day Saints" at Palmyra and vicinity remained faithful, or took more than the first degree in the new institution, is now unknown to the writer. It is recollected that at least a portion, perhaps the majority of them, became backsliders after a very brief experience.

The proposition to publish the new revelation was as yet an adjourned question. Martin Harris enthusiastically favored it, and he was the man calculated on for the means of payment for the printing. He was one of the earliest, if not, in truth, the only real believer. He was a religious monomaniac, reading the Scriptures intently, and could probably repeat from memory nearly every text of the Bible from beginning to end, giving the chapter and verse in each case. His superstition and cupidity were both ap-

* The reader, as he pursues this history, will discover the bearing of the coincidence here referred to, upon the questions of the literary origin and prime invention of the "Golden Bible."

MARTIN HARRIS.

pealed to in this matter. Though he unreservedly gave in his adhesion to the book as of divine appointment, he was by no means so prompt in his willingness to bear the whole cost of printing it, for he was proverbially a covetous, money-loving man, but an honest and benevolent one. His habit had been to look out for the best chances in a bargain, and it was natural that he should desire further opportunity for examination and consideration, and also for trying his influence in proselyting—the latter object being with a view to judging of the question of reimbursement, should he advance the money required—and he was accordingly permitted to take the manuscript translations into his possession. Reading a portion of them to his wife, a Quakeress of positive qualities, she denounced the whole performance as silly and impious. His neighbors and friends, whom he importuned and bored on the subject, uniformly expressed the same sentiment and belief, and cautioned him against being imposed upon and defrauded.

But this opposition served only to strengthen Harris's profession of faith and increase his inclination to make the printing investment. Yet he evidenced some method in his madness, for, before doing so, he sought out the "wisdom of learned men," as he said, relative to the genuineness of the revelation and discovery. He accordingly procured from Smith some resemblances of antique characters or hieroglyphics purporting to be exact copies from the plates; which, together with the translations in his possession, he carried to New York City, where he sought for them the interpretation and bibliological scrutiny of such scholars as Hon. Luther Bradish, Dr. Mitchell, Professor Anthon, and others. All the gentlemen applied to were understood to have scouted the whole pretence as too depraved for serious attention, while commiserating the applicant as the victim of fanaticism or insanity.

Harris, nevertheless, stood firm in his position, regarding these untoward results merely as "proving the lack of wisdom" on the part of the rejecters, and also as illustrating the truth of his favorite quotation, that "God hath chosen the foolish things of the world to confound the wise." This was always his self-convincing argument in reply to similar adversity in his fanatical pursuit.

The following is Professor Anthon's account of Harris's interview with him, as given and published a few years afterward. It was addressed in a letter to a friend in reply to inquiries, and dated

"New York, *February* 17, 1834.

"Some years ago, a plain, apparently simple-hearted farmer, called on me with a note from Dr. Mitchell, of our city, now dead, requesting me to decipher, if possible, the paper which the farmer would hand me. Upon examining the paper in question, I soon came to the conclusion that it was all a trick—perhaps a hoax. When I asked the person who brought it how he obtained the writing, he gave me the following account: A 'golden book,' consisting of a number of plates fastened together by wires of the same material, had been dug up in the northern part of the State of New York, and along with it an enormous pair of 'spectacles!' These spectacles were so large, that, if any person attempted to look through them, his two eyes would look through one glass only—the spectacles in question being altogether too large for the human face, 'Whoever,' he said, 'examined the plates through the glasses, was enabled not only to read them, but fully to understand their meaning.'

"All this knowledge, however, was confined to a young man, who had the trunk containing the book and spectacles in his sole possession. This young man was placed behind a curtain, in a garret in a farm-house, and being thus concealed from view, he put on the spectacles occasionally, or, rather, looked through one of the glasses, deciphered the characters in the book, and having committed some of them to paper, handed copies from behind the curtain to those who stood outside. Not a word was said about their being deciphered by the 'gift of God.' Every thing in this way was effected by the large pair of spectacles. The farmer added, that he had been requested to contribute a sum of money toward the publication of the 'golden book,' the contents of which would, as he was told, produce an entire change in the world, and save it from ruin. So urgent had been these solicitations, that he intended selling his farm and giving the amount to those who wished to publish the plates. As a last precautionary step, he had resolved to come to New York and obtain the opinion of the 'learned' about the meaning of the paper which he had brought with him, and which had been given him as a part of the contents of the book. . . . . . .

"The paper in question was, in fact, a singular scroll. It consisted of all kinds of singular characters, disposed in columns, and had evidently been prepared by some person who had before him at the time a book containing various alphabets; Greek and Hebrew letters, crosses and flourishes, Roman letters inverted or placed sideways, were arranged and placed in perpendicular columns, and the whole ended in a rude delineation of a circle, divided into various compartments, arched with various strange marks, and evidently copied after the Mexican calendar, given by Humboldt, but copied in such a way as not to betray the source whence it was derived. I am thus particular as to the contents of the paper, inasmuch as I have frequently conversed with my friends on the subject since the Mormon excitement began, and well remember that the paper contained any thing else but 'Egyptian hieroglyphics.'

"Yours respectfully,

"CHARLES ANTHON."

Harris appears not to have presented the "translations" with the hieroglyphics to Professor Anthon, or if so, the immaterial fact had left too slight an impression for his recollection at the time of writing the above statement.

The pursuer after knowledge returned home, confirmed rather than shaken in his belief; for he had taken the sensible conclusions of the "learned men" he had seen by the rule of contraries, declaring in a boastful spirit that God had enabled him, an unlearned man as he was, to "confound worldly wisdom." He had apparently become seized with the Golden Bible mania beyond redemption. It was his constant theme wherever he appeared, rendering him, by his readings and commentaries, an object both of sympathy and dread to his friends and all whom he met.

As might have been anticipated, Harris's wife became exceedingly annoyed and disgusted with what she called her husband's "craziness." She foresaw, as she thought, that if he incurred the printing liability, as he had avowed to her his purpose of doing, the event would be the ruin of himself and family.

Thus exercised, she contrived, in her husband's sleep, to steal from him the particular source of her disturbance, and burned the manuscript to ashes. For years she kept this incendiarism a profound secret to herself, even until after the book was published. Smith and Harris held her accountable for the theft, but supposed she had handed the manuscript to some "evil-designing persons" to be used somehow in injuring their cause. A feud was thus produced between husband and wife, which was never reconciled.

Great consternation now pervaded the Mormon circles. The reappearance of the mysterious stranger at Smith's was again the subject of inquiry and conjecture by observers, from whom was withheld all explanation of his identity or purpose. It was not at first an easy task to convince the prophet of the entire innocency of his trusted friend Harris in the matter of this calamitous event, though mutual confidence and friendship were ultimately restored. The great trouble was, the lost translations could not be replaced, or at least such apparently was the difficulty. It might be supposed that, with his golden plates and spectacles before him, and with the benefit of the divine aid as he claimed, the prophet could easily have supplied a duplicate; and so he doubtless would have done had he really been the translator or original author of the composition. To explain his inability to reproduce the missing pages, he said he had received a revelation of the Lord's displeasure for his imprudence in placing them in Harris's hands, and on this account forbidding his rewriting the same; and another reason for this interdiction was, that his enemies had obtained possession of the manuscripts, and altered them with a view of "confounding him" and embarrassing his great work of enlightenment and salvation! He and Harris were undoubtedly led to suppose that the lost manuscripts remained in existence, and might somehow be used for the object assigned.

CHAPTER V.

New Translations—The Prophet's Cave—Printing Contract—Book completed—Harris "pays the Printer."

THE loss of the first translations checked for a time the progress of Mormon events. But Smith, Harris, and their abiding associates were seemingly undismayed. Some six months passed when the announcement was given out that a new and complete translation of the Book of Mormon had been made by the prophet, which was ready for the press. In the interim the stranger before spoken of had again been seen at Smith's; and the prophet had been away from home, may-be to repay the former's visits. The bearing of these circumstances upon any important question can only be left to reasonable conjecture in reference to the subsequent developments. The second manuscripts, like the first, were in Cowdery's handwriting.

The work of translation this time had been done in the recess of a dark artificial cave, which Smith had caused to be dug in the east side of the forest-hill near his residence, now owned by Mr. Amos Miner. At least such was one account given out by the Mormon fraternity; though another version was, that the prophet continued to pursue his former mode of translating behind the curtain at his house, and only went into the cave to pay his spiritual devotions and seek the continued favor of Divine Wisdom. His stays in the cave varied from fifteen minutes to an hour or over—the entrance meanwhile being guarded by one or more of his disciples. This ceremony scarcely attracted the curiosity of outsiders, though it was occasionally witnessed by men and boys living near the scene.

This excavation was at the time said to be one hundred and sixty feet in extent, though that is probably an exaggeration. It had a substantial door of two-inch plank, secured by a corresponding lock. From the lapse of time and natural causes the cave has been closed for years, very little mark of its former existence remaining to be seen.

Encouraged by the continued favoring hallucination of Harris, an active canvass was now commenced by the Mormons for the printing. Harris was the only man of property or credit known in all Mormondom; and, as will appear, he happened to be exactly the appropriate subject for the prophet's designs; for without his timely aid and pecuniary sacrifice the Golden Bible would probably have remained forever an unpublished romance. And, as has already been intimated, he alone was depended upon for the means to pay for its printing, for no other man of the whole Mormon tribe could have raised a dollar of his own money for that or any other object. He was a prosperous, independent farmer, strictly upright in his business dealings, and, although evidencing good qualifications in the affairs of his industrial calling, yet he was the slave of the peculiar religious fanaticism controlling his mental organization. "Marvellousness" being his predominating phrenological development, he was noted for the betrayal of vague superstitions—a belief in dreams, ghosts, hobgoblins, "special providences," terrestrial visits of angels, the interposition of "devils" to afflict sinful men, etc. He was the son of Nathan Harris, an early settler in Palmyra, and aged about forty-three years. His family consisted of a wife, one son, and two daughters.

This was the position of Martin Harris in the community at this important turning-period in his life and career. In June, 1829, Smith the prophet, his brother Hyrum, Cowdery the scribe, and Harris the believer, applied to Mr. Egbert B. Grandin, then publisher of the *Wayne Sentinel* at Palmyra (now deceased), for his price to do the work of one edition of three thousand copies. Harris offered to pay or secure payment if a bargain should be made. Only a few sheets of the manuscript, as a specimen, with the title-page, were exhibited at this time, though the whole number of folios was stated, whereby could be made a calculation of the cost. Mr. Grandin at once expressed his disinclination to entertain the proposal to print at any price, believing the whole affair to be a wicked imposture and a scheme to defraud Mr. Harris, who was his friend, and whom he advised accordingly. This admonition was kindly but firmly resisted by Harris, and resented with assumed pious indignation by the Smiths, Cowdery taking little or no part in the conversation. Some further parleying followed, Harris resolutely persisting in his deafness to the friendly expressions of regard from Mr. Grandin, and also from several other well-disposed neighbors happening to be present at the interview, who vainly united in the effort to dissuade him from his purpose. Afterward, however, it was thought Harris became for a time in some degree staggered in his confidence; but nothing could be done in the way of printing without his aid, and so the prophet persevered in his spell-binding influence and seductive arts, as will be seen, with ultimate success. Further interviews followed, Grandin being earnestly importuned to reconsider his opinion and determination. He was assured by Harris, that if he refused to do the work, it would be procured elsewhere. And the subject was temporarily dropped, except that Grandin complied with Harris's request for an approximate estimate of the cost of the proposed edition.

Immediately thereafter, the same Mormon party, or a portion of them, applied to Mr. Thurlow Weed, of the *Anti-Masonic Inquirer* at Rochester, from whom they met a similar repulse. Mr. Weed's own words in regard to the manuscript and the printing proposal are: "After reading a few chapters, it seemed such a jumble of unintelligible absurdities, that we refused the work, advising Harris not to mortgage his farm and beggar his family." Mr. Elihu F. Marshall, a book publisher, also at Rochester, was then applied to, and he gave his terms for the printing and binding of the book, with his acceptance of the proffered mode of security for the payment.

Whereupon, the "saints" returned to Palmyra, and renewed their request to Mr. Grandin, reassuring him that the work was to be done at any rate, and pleading that they would be saved much inconvenience and cost of travel to have the printing done, at Palmyra, where they lived, especially as the manuscripts were to be delivered and the proof-sheets examined daily by them at the printing-office.

It was upon this statement of the facts, and in this view of the case, that Mr. Grandin, on taking the advice of several discreet, fair-minded neighbors, finally reconsidered his course of policy, and entered into contract for the printing and binding of five thousand copies of the Book of Mormon at the price of $3,000, taking Harris's bond and mortgage as offered in security for payment. The contract was faithfully and satisfactorily fulfilled by both parties, and the book in its entire edition as bargained for was completed and delivered early in the summer of 1830.

In the beginning of the printing the Mormons professed to hold their manuscripts as "sacred," and insisted upon maintaining constant vigilance for their safety during the progress of the work, each morning carrying to the printing-office the instalment required for the day, and withdrawing the same at evening. No alteration from copy in any manner was to be made. These things were "strictly commanded," as they said. Mr. John H. Gilbert, as printer, had the chief operative trust of the type-setting and press-work of the job. After the first day's trial he found the manuscripts in so very imperfect a condition, especially in regard to grammar, that he became unwilling further to obey the "command," and so announced to Smith and his party; when, finally, upon much friendly expostulation, he was given a limited discretion in correcting, which was exercised in the particulars of syntax, orthography, punctuation, capitalizing, paragraphing, etc. Many errors under these heads, nevertheless, escaped correction, as appear in the first edition of the printed book. Very soon, too —after some ten days—the constant vigilance by the

Mormons over the manuscripts was relaxed by reason of the confidence they came to repose in the printers. Mr. Gilbert has now in his possession a complete copy of the book in the original sheets, as laid off by him from the press in working.

It may be due to the memory of Mr. Grandin, in relation to this Golden Bible printing contract, to mention the fact that Mrs. Harris, who had so strenuously objected to her husband's fanatical course, fully conceded the propriety of Mr. Grandin's action under the circumstances as they existed.

Meanwhile, Harris and his wife had separated by mutual arrangement, on account of her persistent unbelief in Mormonism and refusal to be a party to the mortgage. The family estate was divided, Harris giving her about eighty acres of the farm, with a comfortable house and other property as her share of the assets; and she occupied this property until the time of her death. The main farm and homestead, about one hundred and fifty acres of land, was retained by himself, the mortgage covering only this portion; but Mormonism, more than farming or other business, ever afterward engaged his attention, and this was the beginning of adversity which ultimately reduced him to poverty.

The farm mortgaged was sold by Harris in 1831 at private sale, not by foreclosure, and a sufficiency of the avails went to pay Grandin—though it is presumed Harris might have paid the $3,000 without the sale of the farm. This was among the best properties of the kind in the town. Most of it, including the homestead portion, is the same now owned by Mr. Thomas Chapman, a mile and a half north of the village of Palmyra.

As will be seen, Harris was led to believe that the book would be a profitable speculation for him, and very likely in this may be traced his leading motive for taking the venture. He was vouchsafed the security of a "special revelation" commanding that the new Bible should in no instance be sold at a less price than "ten shillings," and that he himself should have the exclusive right of sale, with all the avails—the only purpose of the Mormon saints being the unselfish one to "get the great light before the world for the salvation of mankind!" Indeed, he figured up the profits with all the certainty of their realization, that the most enthusiastic calculator would feel in "counting his chickens before they are hatched." Like thousands of fortunes made on paper, this process by Harris was an easy matter, thus: 5,000 books at $1.25 per book, $6,250. First cost, $3,000. Showing a clear speculation of over one hundred per cent. upon the investment!

In October following (1829), the printing was considerably advanced, and the ultimate issue of the Book of Mormon had become a fixed fact. The printing was done upon a hand-press, and the type of one form had to be distributed before another could be set up; and of course this will account for the tardiness of the work. But the first and second books of "Nephi," and some other portions of the forthcoming revelation, were printed in sheets;—and armed with a copy of these, Smith commenced other preparations for a mission to Pennsylvania, where he had some relatives residing, and where the before-mentioned "Rev. Sidney Rigdon" was then residing or temporarily sojourning. His wardrobe needed replenishing, and Harris, who was abundantly able to do as he did, and withal counting on his prospective profits in the bible speculation, procured for him a new black suit, remarking to the merchant of whom he bought the cloth, that as the prophet was going on a mission to preach the new gospel, it was necessary that he should "appear comely before men;" and consequently ordered the best pattern in the store. Mr. David S. Aldrich, now a prominent dry-goods merchant in Palmyra, sold the cloth as a clerk at that time. The result was, that in November, Smith went to Northern Pennsylvania, as previously appointed, where he married the daughter of Isaac Hale, and was baptized after the Mormon ritual—Rigdon being the "matchmaker" and the officiating "clergyman" in these celebrations. Mr. Hale, the father-in-law, never became a Mormon.

Smith soon returned to Palmyra, to complete his grand design, having made on this occasion, so far as known, no sensation as a preacher, nor any progress in his proselyting mission beyond his nuptial capture.

CHAPTER VI.

Publication of the Mormon Bible—Blooming of the Church of Latter-Day Saints—Its Patriarch and President—Characteristic Anecdote—Failure of "Golden Bible" Speculation.

THE newly revealed gospel having been opened to the world in a printed book, Prophet Smith and his disciples proceeded to a more perfect organization of their church for its practice and dissemination. This ceremony, conducted with apparent seriousness by the prophet, supported on the right and left by Cowdery and Harris—of which it is now too late to give the full particulars from memory—took place in the dwelling-house of Joseph Smith, Sr., in the month of June, 1830. There was no praying, singing, or preaching attempted, but Joseph gave various readings and interpretations of the new bible. The senior Smith was installed "Patriarch and President of the Church of Latter-Day Saints;" while Cowdery and Harris were nominated vicegerents to the prophet, or dignitaries of equivalent import, and a limited commission of priesthood and prophecy was conferred upon them by the prophet, accompanied by the "laying on of hands" and other ceremonious observances, adding great "promises" of future spiritual endowment, to depend in an essential manner on their fidelity and efficiency in the trust already reposed in them.

The participants generally in this incipient church inauguration were the individuals named as the pioneer saints in a preceding chapter, with perhaps few changes *pro* and *con.* The rite of baptism by immersion was administered by the prophet to Cowdery and Harris at their particular request—a pool for that purpose having been created by constructing a dam across the brook near the place of meeting; and then the other baptisms on this occasion were conducted by Cowdery, including in these benefits both the aged parents of the revelator, Page, Mrs. Rockwell, Dolly Proper, and several of the Whitmer brothers. So far as can be recollected of the proceedings, as verbally reported at the time, no others were then baptized; but afterward this baptismal service was extended to all the saints who had not already been the favored subjects of that ritual, Cowdery continuing to officiate in these solemnities.

The prophet himself was not baptized in this instance, the explanation of the omission being, as stated by some of the faithful, that he was elevated far above "worldly baptism" by reason of his "spiritual sphere;" but another account—doubtless the accepted one—assigned as the reason in the case that he had previously received the ordinance in Pennsylvania by the ministration of "Brother Rigdon," and was the first Mormon baptized since the times of the primitive Nephites.

A few days after this preliminary launching of the Mormon ship Zion—this primeval foundation of the Mormon theocracy—some ten or twelve of the saints went to Fayette, in an adjoining county, where similar observances were had in the formation of a church. There were about thirty persons in attendance on this occasion, believers and spectators, and a number of new converts were reported, Cowdery again performing the baptismal service. But, finally, it was found that the prophet's own country was an unfavorable locality for success in this wonderful religious speculation; the new gospel was held in light repute by the "Gentile" people; conversions did not come up to the anticipations of the leaders; and in the course of the same year these pioneer Mormons emigrated to Ohio.

Now, let the reader's attention be carried back to the commencement of the Golden Bible publication. The book, as a money-making enterprise, fell dead before the public. As a religious demonstration, it was received by the community as "stale, flat, and fulsome." It was repulsive to the popular common-sense, and, beyond the minds of its preëxistent devotees, simply awakened contempt and ridicule. It found no buyers, or but very few. So that the glittering visions of Harris and others, who might have thought as he had done, seemed to turn out as illusory as had been those of Smith's money-digging dupes. Hence another "command" became necessary in regard to the sale of the book, after a few weeks' faithful but unsuccessful trial of the market by Harris as a monopolist salesman.* This was easily called down by Smith in favor of his patriarch father. Time passed, and yet the disappointment was unalleviated. The patriarch having been permitted by this changed revelation, with the consent of Harris, to appropriate a portion of the avails of sales toward his family necessities, he effected some sales, chiefly in barter trades, on accommodating terms for the purchasers of the books, always nominally maintaining the revealed price of ten shillings, to avoid the awful penalty of "instant death" for any departure from it. Pedes-

* Harris was proverbially a peaceful as well as an honest man. He was slow to retaliate an offence. The following anecdote will show what manner of man he was. Urging the sale of the book with pertinacious confidence in the genuineness of the Smith revelation, he fell into debate about its character with a neighbor of an irascible temperament. His opponent became angry, and struck him a severe blow upon the right side of his face. Instantly turning toward the assailant the other cheek, he quoted the Christian maxim, reading it from the book in his hand, page 481 (as it also appears in Matthew): "Whosoever shall smite thee on the right cheek, turn to him the other also."

trian peddling jaunts were made in the neighboring villages and surrounding country, and books peddled off by him in exchange for various articles of farmers' produce and shop merchandise, such as "wouldn't come amiss for family use in hard times." In this way considerable improvement was made in the old "saint's" exchequer. Harris, meanwhile, seemed to stand firm in his adhesion to the book's divinity, and always had at his tongue's end an amplitude of scriptural and Mormonic quotations of "promises," giving satisfactory assurance of his ultimate pecuniary and spiritual salvation.

Many appropriate incidents might be related from the memory of individuals yet living at the original scene of this blooming of the Mormon Church, illustrative of the shallowness of the great imposture; but which, given in detail, would surfeit the reader's curiosity. A single anecdote will suffice to show the degree of sincerity attached to the pretended "commandment price" of the book.

The Patriarch and President of the Mormon Church was now preparing to remove with his family to Ohio, where the Prophet Joseph and his brother Hyrum, with others of the faith, had already preceded them, and it was necessary to procure some articles of outfit. In pursuance of this object, he took a basket of "bibles" in his hand and walked to Palmyra village, where he had usually done his small traffic, and where sundry unadjusted little scores were ready to confront him, which his overplus book avails and other resources had been insufficient to liquidate. By the then prevailing legal system for the collection of debts (residing, as he did, over the county line from Palmyra), he made himself liable to suit by warrant and also detention in imprisonment for non-payment. But necessity being his master, he had taken the incautious venture, and soon found himself in the constable's custody at the suit of a creditor for a small book account. The parties appeared before A. R. Tiffany, Esq., a justice of the peace for Wayne County, by whom the warrant had been issued. After some preliminary parleying by the debtor, he invited and enjoyed a private interview with the creditor in an adjoining room. The debt and costs had now reached the aggregate of $5.63. The embarrassments in the case, after some brief discussion, were found to be of a difficult nature. At last, laying the good-natured claimant under strict confidential injunction, and referring with solemn air to the "command" by which he was empowered to sell his Mormon work only at the price of $1.25 per copy, the crafty "patriarch" proposed, nevertheless, on the express condition that his perfidy should not be exposed, the offer of seven books in full for the demand, being a fraction more than eighty cents apiece. The joke was relished as too good to go unpatronized, and though the books were not regarded as possessing any value, the claimant, more in a spirit of mischief than otherwise, accepted the compromise accordingly. The *finale* was, that the Mormon saint was permitted to slip home from a side door, to avoid like importunities from other creditors, and it is believed this was his last appearance in Palmyra by daylight.

Such was the advent, and such the popular reception of the Book of Mormon, and the Church of the Latter-Day Saints founded thereon as its corner-stone, at the place of their professed origin. The book has since gone through many editions in the different languages of the civilized world. The title-page is as follows:

"THE

"BOOK OF MORMON;

"AN ACCOUNT WRITTEN BY THE HAND OF MORMON, UPON PLATES TAKEN FROM THE PLATES OF NEPHI.

"Wherefore it is an abridgment of the Record of the people of Nephi; and also of the Lamanites; written to the Lamanites, which are a remnant of the House of Israel; and also to Jew and Gentile; written by way of commandment, and also by the spirit of Prophecy and of Revelation. Written, and sealed up, and hid up unto the Lord, that they might not be destroyed; to come forth by the gift and power of God unto the interpretation thereof; sealed by the hand of Moroni, and hid up unto the Lord, to come forth in due time by the way of Gentile; the interpretation thereof by the gift of God: an abridgment taken from the Book of Ether.

"Also, which is a Record of the People of Jared, which were scattered at the time the Lord confounded the language of the people when they were building a tower to get to Heaven; which is to show unto the remnant of the House of Israel how great things the Lord hath done for their fathers; and that they may know the covenants of the Lord, that they are not cast off forever; and also to the convincing of the Jew and Gentile that Jesus is the Christ, the External God, manifesting Himself unto all nations. And now if there be fault, it be the mistake of men; wherefore condemn not the things of God, that ye may be found spotless at the judgment-seat of Christ.

"By JOSEPH SMITH, Junior,
"Author and Proprietor.

"Palmyra:
"Printed by E. B. Grandin, for the Author.
"1830."

In revised editions as printed at Nauvoo and Salt Lake, the *prima facie* inconsistency of styling Smith the "*Author* and Proprietor" of the book, as above seen to have been originally assumed, is removed by denominating him as "Translator" only. The first edition also contained a precautionary "preface" in reference to the lost translations before mentioned, which is omitted in the revised editions. It is in the following words:

"TO THE READER—

"As many false reports have been circulated respecting the following work, and also many unlawful measures taken by evil-designing persons to destroy me, and also the work, I would inform you that I translated, by the gift and power of God, and caused to be written, one hundred and sixteen pages, the which I took from the Book of Lehi, which was an account abridged from the plates of Lehi, by the hand of Mormon; which said account, some person or persons have stolen and kept from me, notwithstanding my utmost exertions to recover it again—and being commanded of the Lord that I should not translate the same over again, for Satan had put it into their hearts to tempt the Lord their God, by altering the words, that they did read contrary from that which I translated and caused to be written; and if I should bring forth the same words again, or, in other words, if I should translate the same over again, they would publish that which they had stolen, and Satan would stir up the hearts of this generation, that they might not receive this work: but behold, the Lord said unto me, I will not suffer that Satan shall accomplish his evil design in this thing; therefore thou shalt translate from the plates of Nephi, until ye come to that which ye have translated, which ye have retained; and behold, ye shall publish it as the record of Nephi; and thus I will confound those who have altered my words. I will not suffer that they shall destroy my work; yea, I will show unto them that my wisdom is greater than the cunning of the devil. Wherefore, to be obedient unto the commandments of God, I have, through His grace and mercy, accomplished that which he hath commanded me respecting this thing. I would also inform you that the plates of which hath been spoken, were found in the township of Manchester, Ontario County, New York.

"THE AUTHOR."

This Mormon revelation is divided into various books, which are here given in the order as they appear in the printed work, viz.: "The First Book of Nephi, his Reign and Ministry," seven chapters; "The Second Book of Nephi," fifteen chapters; "The Book of Jacob, the Brother of Nephi," five chapters; "The Book of Enos," one chapter; "The Book of Jarom," one chapter; "The Book of Omni," one chapter; "The Words of Mormon," one chapter; "The Book of Mosiah," thirteen chapters; "The Book of Alma, the Son of Alma," thirty chapters; "The Book of Heleman," five chapters; "The Book of Nephi, the Son of Nephi, which was the Son of Helaman," fourteen chapters; "The Book of Nephi, which is the Son of Nephi, one of the Disciples of Jesus Christ," one chapter; "Book of Mormon," four chapters; "Book of Ether," six chapters; "Book of Moroni," ten chapters. The volume contains five hundred and eighty-eight pages, common duodecimo, small pica letter.

CHAPTER VII.

Modified Revelation—Testimony of Witnesses—A Prophet that was not a Prophet—Sidney Rigdon the first regular Preacher of the new Gospel—His Sermon—Calvin Stoddard receives a "Call"—Mormon Emigration to Ohio.

SMITH's first "command" limiting to his eye alone the mortal sight of the metallic records, except on the penalty of "instant death" denounced against the daring of any other human being, failed in its apparent purpose. It was treated as "Joe's nonsense" outside of the immediate circle of his small band of followers, as were all his stories of visions and of the "golden" book. Hence a modification of the revelation seemingly became necessary to secure the public acceptance of this miraculous spiritual dispensation. Exactly when this change was reached, did not generally transpire, or at least it is not within remembrance, though for months antecedent to the publication of the book, the conclusive "testimony of witnesses" to the actual sight and veritable existence of "the plates which contained the record," was verbally proclaimed by Smith and others in corroboration of the prophetic pretension. This circumstance explains the otherwise apparent inconsistency of the following allegations of eleven witnesses, which are appended to the printed volume:

"*The Testimony of three Witnesses:*

"Be it known unto all nations, kindreds, tongues, and people, unto whom this work shall come, that we, through the grace of God the Father and our Lord Jesus Christ, have seen the plates which contain this record, which is a record of the people of Nephi, and also of the Lamanites, his brethren, and also of the people of Jared, which came from the tower of which hath been spoken; and we also know that they have been translated by the gift and power of God, for His voice hath declared it unto us; wherefore we know of a surety that the work is true. And we also testify that we have seen the engravings which are upon the plates; and they have been shown unto us by the power of God, and not of man. And we declare with words of soberness, that an angel of God came down from Heaven, and he brought and laid before our eyes, that we beheld and saw the plates, and the engravings thereon; and we know that it is by the grace of God the Father, and our Lord Jesus Christ, that we beheld and bare record that these things are true; and it is marvellous in our eyes: nevertheless, the voice of the Lord commanded us that we should bear record of it; wherefore, to be obèdient unto the commandments of God, we bear testimony of these things. And we know that if we are faithful in Christ, we shall rid our garments of the blood of all men, and be found spotless before the judgment-seat of Christ, and shall dwell with Him eternally in the heavens. And the honor be to the Father, and to the Son, and to the Holy Ghost, which is one God. Amen.

OLIVER COWDERY,
DAVID WHITMER,
MARTIN HARRIS."

"*And also the Testimony of eight Witnesses:*

"Be it known unto all nations, kindreds, tongues, and people, unto whom this work shall come, that Joseph Smith, Jr., the Author and Proprietor of this work, has shown unto us the plates of which hath been spoken, which have the appearance of gold; and as many of the leaves as the said Smith has translated we did handle with our hands; and we also saw the engravings thereon, all of which has the appearance of ancient work, and of curious workmanship. And this we bear record, with words of soberness, that the said Smith has shown unto us, for we have seen and hefted, and know of a surety, that the said Smith has got the plates of which we have spoken. And we give our names unto the world, to witness unto the world that which we have seen: and we lie not, God bearing witness of it.

CHRISTIAN WHITMER,
JACOB WHITMER,
PETER WHITMER, Jr.,
JOHN WHITMER,
HIRAM PAGE,
JOSEPH SMITH, Sr.,
HYRUM SMITH,
SAMUEL H. SMITH."

How to reconcile the act of Harris in signing his name to such a statement, in view of the character of honesty which had always been conceded to him, could never be easily explained. In reply to uncharitable suggestions of his neighbors, he used to practise a good deal of his characteristic jargon about "seeing with the spiritual eye," and the like. As regards the other witnesses associated with Harris, their averments in this or any other matter could excite no more surprise than did those of Smith himself.

It is interesting to quote the standard of Mormon authority for the justification of Smith's changed revelation which opened the way for these witnesses to sustain the existence of the metallic records. Here it is, as recorded in the eleventh chapter of the "Second Book of Nephi":

"And it shall come to pass, that the Lord God shall bring forth unto you, the words of a book, and they shall be the words of them which have slumbered. And behold the book shall be sealed: and in the book shall be a revelation from God, from the beginning of the world to the ending thereof. Wherefore, because of the things which are sealed up, the things which are sealed shall not be delivered in the day of the wickedness and abominations of the people. Wherefore the book shall be kept from them. But the book shall be delivered unto a man, and he shall deliver the words of the book, which are the words of those who have slumbered in the dust; and he shall deliver these words unto another; but the words which are sealed he shall not deliver, neither shall he deliver the book. For the book shall be sealed by the power of God, and the revelation which was sealed, shall be kept in the book until the own due time of the Lord, that they may come forth; for, behold, they reveal all things from the foundation of the world unto the end thereof. And the day cometh that the words of the book which were sealed shall be read upon the house-tops; and they shall be read by the power of Christ: and all things shall be revealed unto the children of men which ever have been among the children of men, and which ever will be, even unto the end of the earth. Wherefore, at that day when the book shall be delivered unto the man of whom I have spoken, the book shall be hid from the eyes of the world, that the eyes of none shall behold it, save it be that three witnesses shall behold it, by the power of God, besides him to whom the book shall be delivered; and they shall testify to the truth of the book and the things therein. And there is none other which shall view it, save it be a few, according to the will of God, to bear testimony of His word unto the children of men: for the Lord God hath said, that the words of the faithful should speak as if it were from the dead. Wherefore, the Lord God will proceed to bring forth the words of the book; and in the mouth of as many witnesses as seemeth Him good, will He establish His word; and woe be unto him that rejecteth the Word of God.

"But behold, it shall come to pass that the Lord God shall say unto him to whom He shall deliver the book, Take these words which are not sealed, and deliver them to another, that he may show them unto the learned, saying: Read this, I pray thee. And the learned shall say, Bring hither the book, and I will read them; and now, because of the glory of the world, and to get gain, will they say this, and not for the glory of God. And the man shall say, I cannot bring the book, for it is sealed. Then shall the learned say, I cannot read it. Wherefore it shall come to pass that the Lord God will deliver again the book and the words thereof to him that is not learned; and the man that is not learned shall say, I am not learned. Then shall the Lord God say unto him, The learned shall not read them, for they have rejected them, and I am able to do mine own work; wherefore thou shalt read the words which I shall give unto thee. Touch not the things which are sealed, for I will bring them forth in mine own due time: for I will show unto the children of men that I am able to do mine own work. Wherefore, when thou hast read the words which I have commanded thee, and obtained the witnesses which I have promised unto thee, then shalt thou seal up the book again, and hide it up unto me, that I may preserve the words which thou hast not read, until I shall see fit in mine own wisdom to reveal all things unto the children of men. For behold, I am God; and I am a God of miracles; and I will show unto the world that I am the same yesterday, to-day, and forever; and I work not among the children of men, save it be according to their faith."

Another theory in regard to the plates and hieroglyphics claimed to be found by Smith may possibly be explained in this way. In the list of American antiquities found in the Western country, and preserved in the museums of antiquarians, are what are called *glyphs*, consisting of curious metallic plates covered with hieroglyphical characters. Professor Rafinesque, in his *Asiatic Journal* for 1832, describes similar plates found by him in Mexico, being "written from top to bottom like the Chinese, or from side to side indifferently, like the Egyptian and the Demotic Libyan." A number of these remains were found a few years ago in Pike County, Illinois, described as "six plates of brass of a bell shape, each having a hole near the small end, with a ring through all of them, and clasped with two clasps. The ring and clasps appeared to be iron, very much oxidated. The plates first appeared to be copper, and had the appearance of being covered with characters. A cleansing by sulphuric acid brought out the characters distinctly." Smith may have obtained through Rigdon (the literary genius behind the screen) one of these glyphs, which resemble so nearly his description of the book he pretended to find on Mormon Hill. For the credit of human character, it is better at any rate to presume this, and that the eleven ignorant witnesses were deceived by appearances, than to conclude that they wilfully committed such gross moral perjury before high Heaven, as their solemn averments imply.

Mormonism and its bible being thus candidates for acceptance or rejection before the public judgment, an early popular decision was sought by their supporters. Up to this time, Sidney Rigdon had played his part in the background, and his occasional visits at Smith's residence had been noticed by uninitiated observers as those of the mysterious stranger. It had been his policy to remain in concealment until all things should be in readiness for blowing the trumpet of the new gospel. He was a backsliding clergyman of the Baptist persuasion, and at the period referred to was the principal preacher of a sort of religious society calling themselves "Reformers" or "Disciples," at Mentor, Ohio, near Kirtland. From all that is known by the writer, of his character, he is believed to have been a man possessing considerable educational and scientific abilities; an active, sanguineous temperament; a bold and persevering disposition; and inclinations preponderating toward original theories and schemes of philosophical adventure. His age at this period was about thirty-eight years.

This man Rigdon now appeared as the first regular Mormon preacher in Palmyra. Martin Harris was his forerunner, and relieved him of his incognito position. Harris had in vain sought the use of the churches respectively for his appointed clerical service. But the hall of the Palmyra Young Men's Association, in the third story of Exchange Row, was yielded for the object, upon the earnest entreaty of Harris, whose sincerity and good intentions were unquestioned. At the designated hour, a respectable audience had assembled; but it was a small one, for be it remembered that the church of the order of Latter-Day Saints was just emerging from its chrysalis state.

Rigdon introduced himself as "the Messenger of

SIDNEY RIGDON IN HIS FIRST MORMON SERMON.

God," declaring that he was commanded from above to proclaim the Mormon revelation. He then went through the ceremonious form of prayer, in which he expressed his grateful sense of the blessings of the glorious gospel dispensation now opening to the world, and the miraculous light from Heaven to be displayed through the instrumentality of the "chosen revelator," Joseph Smith, Jr. Bespeaking the favor of the Most High in return for the kindness of the Association in granting the use of their hall, he concluded his prayer by commending all believers to the divine care and protection against the sneers and persecutions of their adversaries.

The discourse was based upon the following text read by the preacher from the recently published Book of Mormon, which the searcher may find in "First Book of Nephi," chapter iv. (page 32, original edition):—

"And the angel spake unto me, saying: These last records which thou hast seen among the Gentiles, shall establish the truth of the first, which is of the Twelve Apostles of the Lamb, and shall make known the plain and precious things which have been taken away from them; and shall make known to all kindreds, tongues, and people, that the Lamb of God is the Eternal Father and Saviour of the world; and that all men must come unto Him, or they cannot be saved."

The preacher assumed to establish the theory that the Book of Mormon and the old Bible were one in inspiration and importance, and that the "precious things" now revealed had for wise purposes been withheld from the book first promulgated to the world, and were necessary to establish its truth. In the course of his argument he applied various quotations from the two books to prove his position. Holding the Book of Mormon in his right hand, and the Bible in his left hand, he brought them together in a manner corresponding to the emphatic declaration made by him, that they were both equally the Word of God; that neither was perfect without the other; and that they were inseparably necessary to complete the everlasting gospel of the Saviour Jesus Christ. The "latter-day" theory was dwelt upon at some length, with apparent seriousness. Reiterating the declaration made in his introduction, that he was "commanded" to proclaim these truths for the salvation of fallen man, he wound up his discourse by a warning appeal to the confidence and faith of his hearers; adding a benediction.

This is by no means offered as a literal report of the "sermon" beyond a few points, but is believed to state truthfully and fairly its essential features, as quite distinctly remembered after the lapse of nearly thirty-seven years. Altogether, though evidencing some talent and ingenuity in its matter and manner, and delivered with startling boldness and seeming sincerity, the performance was in the main an unintelligible jumble of quotations, assertions, and obscurities, which was received by the audience as shockingly blasphemous, as it was painful to hear. The manifestations of disfavor were so unequivocal that Harris hesitatingly assented to the suggestion of his "Gentile" friends to withhold all further request for the use of the hall for a repetition of the exhibition. And "regular preaching" upon the Mormon plan was never again attempted by Rigdon or any other man in Palmyra, according to the best knowledge and belief of the writer.

Rigdon, however, remained at Smith's for some days, preaching in the neighborhood, and baptizing several converts. Smith himself, with Harris, Cowdery, and Stoddard, also made some advances toward preaching in an irregular, miscellaneous way, in barns and in the streets; but all these failed to find "orderly-behaved" hearers in sufficient numbers to encourage their persistence in the clerical vocation. They "lacked the gift of public speaking" to communicate the revelation, as was explained by themselves. Cowdery excelled in the baptismal service, but that seemed to be the extent of his ministerial talent.

An anecdote, well remembered by numerous people now living near the scene of the performance, will serve as an illustration of the facility with which Smith gained converts and co-laborers.

Stoddard was an early believer in Mormonism, and was quite as eccentric a character as Harris. He was slightly impressed that he had a call to preach the new gospel, but his mind was beclouded with perplexing doubts upon the question. One dark night, about ten o'clock, Stephen S. Harding, then a stalwart, fun-loving, dare-devil genius of eighteen years, late Territorial Governor of Utah (not a Mormon), who well knew Stoddard's peculiarities, and being bent on making a sensation, repaired with his genial friend, Abner Tucker, to the residence of the enthusiast; and awakening him from sleep by three signals upon the door with a huge stone, deliberately proclaimed, in a loud, sonorous voice, with solemn intonations—"C-a-l-v-i-n S-t-o-d-d-a-r-d! t-h-e a-n-g-e-l o-f t-h-e Lo-r-d c-o-m-m-a-n-d-s t-h-a-t b-e-f-o-r-e a-n-o-t-h-e-r g-o-i-n-g d-o-w-n o-f t-h-e s-u-n, t-h-o-u s-h-a-l-t g-o f-o-r-t-h a-m-o-n-g t-h-e p-e-o-p-l-e a-n-d p-r-e-a-c-h t-h-e g-o-s-p-e-l o-f N-e-p-h-i, o-r t-h-y w-i-f-e s-h-a-l-l b-e a w-i-d-o-w, t-h-y c-h-i-l-d-r-e-n o-r-p-h-a-n-s, a-n-d t-h-y a-s-h-e-s s-c-a-t-t-e-r-e-d t-o t-h-e f-o-u-r w-i-n-d-s o-f h-e-a-v-e-n!"

The experiment was a complete success. Stoddard's former convictions were now confirmed. Such a convincing "revelation" was final, and not to be disregarded. Early the next morning the subject of this "special call" was seen upon his rounds among his neighbors, as a Mormon missionary, earnestly telling them of the "command" he had received to preach. Luminous arguments and evidences were adduced by him to sustain the foundation of his belief in this his revealed sphere of duty!

In further illustration of the strange superstitions characterizing these pioneer disciples of Mormonism, and to complete the chain of facts going to make up this truthful history, it is proper to add one other important incident, which has never appeared in any accepted record of the saints. Enthusiastic members of the brotherhood—perhaps it should be said the more visionary of the believers—had plied the "spirit of prophecy" in foretelling the event of a miraculous birth in association with an unmarried daughter of Joseph Smith, Sr. This predicted event was to astonish the gentile world as a second advent of triune humanity. Harris was exceedingly happy in the belief of a forthcoming prophet or Messiah under the Mormon dispensation, and spoke unreservedly of an "immaculate conception in our day and generation." The ample shrewdness of the prophet had probably been called in requisition to allay some unfavorable surmises on the part of his observing disciple, who was a frequenter at the family mansion; and it is apparent that the theory invented was readily adopted by Harris. Rigdon had been an occasional sojourner

4*

at Smith's for a year or more, though the reader may fail to perceive what this circumstance had to do with the case. The upshot of the story is, that soon after the family had started for Ohio, the miracle eventuated somewhere on the route, in the birth of a lifeless female child! The *accident* was readily set down to the account of divine interposition to avenge some act of Mormon disobedience, and Harris was thus easily reconciled.

In the summer of 1830, the founders of the Mormon Church then remaining at the scene of its birthplace, who had talked much of going on a mission into the Western country to convert the Lamanites (meaning Indians), started on their western expedition with their unsold Golden Bibles, and went to Mentor, Ohio, the residence of Rigdon, and of Parley P. Pratt, his friend and co-worker. Near this place is Kirtland, where there were a few families belonging to Rigdon's congregation, who had become extremely fanatical under his preparatory preaching and prophecies, and were daily looking for the occurrence of some wonderful event. Seventeen of these people, men and women, readily espoused the new revelation, and were immersed by Cowdery in one night, in attestation of their Mormon faith. By the continued ministration of Rigdon, aided by Pratt, Smith, Cowdery, and their auxiliaries, conversions rapidly followed; a powerful impetus was given to the cause; and over one hundred persons were added to the fold in a short time. Kirtland from about this period became the headquarters of the Mormons, where their Church and colony were thoroughly organized and temporarily established.

CHAPTER VIII.

Style of the new Revelation—Passages from the Book—Scattered Tribes—Journey from Jerusalem to the Promised Land—Their Tribulations in the Wilderness and at Sea—Records "hid up in the Hill Camorah" or Mormon Hill.

Although the Book of Mormon has a wide publicity—being received as authentic by the followers of the late prophet, Smith, and of his successor Brigham Young—and having been issued in large editions, both by the "saints" as their bible, and by "gentiles" on speculation, yet it is presumed that liberal transcripts from the work will compensate their reprinting in this volume. And it may be proper to remark here, that in this case no trespass is perpetrated upon the copyright of 1829 (if indeed the patent is continued by renewals), for the proposed republication is only an adjourned exercise of privilege verbally granted at that time by the "author and proprietor" himself.

The chief denominations of the fabulous tribes purporting to have inhabited this wilderness continent in the times of the first Mormon, according to the Smith revelation, were the Nephites and the Lamanites. They were exceedingly belligerent races of people, apparently bent on each other's destruction, and prosecuting an almost continuous warfare between themselves for century after century; and this, too, so far as assigned, for causes about as explicable as are those impelling like hostilities in this modern Christian era. A melancholy history on this head is presented in the book, from which it appears that the Nephite tribes, though the better people, were eventually annihilated; while to the wandering tribes of the native Indians of this country are to be traced the surviving remnants of their enemies the Lamanites.

By the following series of compilations from the different chapters of this Mormon volume, as translated and published by Prophet Smith, the reader will discover a chain of events, incidents, episodes, perils, and tribulations, by wilderness and by sea, constituting the story of immigration by various Israelitish tribes, with their brazen and golden records, from the beginning of their journeyings at Jerusalem, to the consummation of the same in the promised land, where their records were hidden in the "hill Camorah," which being interpreted, signifies "Mormon Hill," in the town of Manchester, N. Y. The fabulous narrative will repay patient perusal by the curious:

Journeyings of Nephi and his brethren from Jerusalem to the Promised Land, with their records and history. Also, Laman and his brethren.

"I, Nephi, having been born of goodly parents, therefore I was taught somewhat in all the learning of my father; and having seen many afflictions in the course of my days—nevertheless, having been highly favored of the Lord in all my days; yea, having had a great knowledge of the goodness and the mysteries of God, therefore I make a record of my proceedings in my days; yea, I make a record in the language of my father, which consists of the learning of the Jews and the language of the Egyptians. And I know the record which I make to be true; and I make it with mine own hand; and I make it according to my knowledge.

"For it came to pass, in the commencement of the first year of the reign of Zedekiah, king of Judah, (my father Lehi having dwelt at Jerusalem in all his days,) and in that same year there came many prophets, prophesying unto the people that they must repent, or the great city Jerusalem must be destroyed. Wherefore it came to pass that my father Lehi, as he went forth, prayed unto the Lord, yea, even with all his heart, in behalf of his people.

"And it came to pass as he prayed unto the Lord,

there came a pillar of fire and dwelt upon a rock before him, and he saw and heard much; and because of the things which he saw and heard he did quake and tremble exceedingly.

"And it came to pass that he returned to his own house at Jerusalem; and he cast himself upon his bed, being overcome with the spirit and the things which he had seen; and being thus overcome with the spirit, he was carried away in a vision, even that he saw the heavens open; and he thought he saw God sitting upon his throne, surrounded with numberless concourses of angels in the attitude of singing and praising their God.

"And it came to pass that he saw one descending out of the midst of heaven, and he beheld that his lustre was above that of the sun at noonday; and he also saw twelve others following him, and their brightness did exceed that of the stars in the firmament; and they came down and went forth upon the face of the earth; and the first came and stood before my father and gave unto him a book, and bade him that he should read.

"And it came to pass that as he read, he was filled with the spirit of the Lord, and he read, saying: Woe, woe unto Jerusalem! for I have seen thine abominations; yea, and many things did my father read concerning Jerusalem; that it should be destroyed, and the inhabitants thereof; many should perish by the sword, and many should be carried away captive into Babylon. . . . . . .

"And it came to pass that the Lord spake unto me, saying: Blessed art thou, Nephi, because of thy faith, for thou hast sought me diligently, with lowliness of heart. And inasmuch as ye shall keep my commandments, ye shall prosper, and shall be led to a land of promise; yea, even a land which I have prepared for you; yea, a land which is choice above all other lands. . . . . . .

"And I, Nephi, and my brethren, took our journey in the wilderness with our tents, to go up to the land of Jerusalem. And it came to pass that when we had come up to the land of Jerusalem, I and my brethren did consult one with another; and we cast lots which of us should go in unto the house of Laban. And it came to pass that the lot fell upon Laman; and Laman went in unto the house of Laban, and he talked with him as he sat in his house. And he desired of Laban the records which were engraven upon the plates of brass * which contained the genealogy of my father.

* In other portions of the book, plates of *gold* are spoken of. For instance, in the "Book of Mosiah," occurs this passage: "Therefore he took the records which were engraven on the plates of brass, and also the plates of Nephi, and all the things which he had kept and preserved, according to the commandments of God, after having translated and caused to be written the records which were on the

"And behold, it came to pass that Laban was angry, and thrust him out from his presence; and he would not that he should have the records. . . .

"And behold, it is wisdom in God that we should obtain these records, that we might preserve unto our children the language of our fathers; and also that we may preserve unto them the words which have been spoken by the mouth of all the holy prophets, which have been delivered unto them by the spirit and power of God since the world began, even down unto this present time.

"And it came to pass, that after this manner of language did I persuade my brethren that they might be faithful in keeping the commandments of God. And it came to pass that we went down to the land of our inheritance, and we did gather together our gold, and our silver, and our precious things. And after that we had gathered these things together, we went up again unto the house of Laban.

"And it came to pass that we went in unto Laban, and desired him that he would give unto us the records which were engraven upon the plates of brass, for which we would give unto him our gold, and our silver, and our precious things. . . . . .

"And after that they had given thanks unto the

PLATES OF GOLD," etc. In the first instance, these plates or glyphs, or *myths*, were claimed by Smith and his followers to be plates of gold or resembling gold.

God of Israel, my father Lehi took the records which were engraven upon the plates of brass, and he did search them from the beginning. And he beheld that they did contain the five books of Moses, which gave an account of the creation of the world, and also of Adam and Eve, which were our first parents; and also a record of the Jews from the beginning, even down to the commencement of the reign of Zedekiah, king of Judah; and also the prophecies of the holy prophets, from the beginning even down to the commencement of the reign of Zedekiah; and also many prophecies of which have been spoken by the mouth of Jeremiah.

"And it came to pass that my father Lehi also found upon the plates of brass a genealogy of his father; yea, even that Joseph which was the son of Jacob, which was sold into Egypt, and which was preserved by the hand of the Lord, that he might preserve his father Jacob and all his household from perishing with famine. And they were also led out of captivity and out of the land of Egypt by that same God who had preserved them. And thus my father Lehi did discover the genealogy of his fathers. And Laban also was a descendant of Joseph, wherefore he and his fathers had kept the records.

"And now when my father saw all these things, he was filled with the spirit, and began to prophesy concerning his seed; that these plates of brass should go forth unto all nations, kindreds, tongues, and people, which were of his seed. Wherefore he said that these plates of brass should never perish; neither should they be dimmed any more by time. And he prophesied many things concerning his seed.

"And it came to pass that thus far I and my father had kept the commandments wherewith the Lord had commanded us. And we had obtained the records which the Lord had commanded us, and searched them and found that they were desirable; yea, even of great worth unto us, insomuch that we could preserve the commandments of the Lord unto our children. Wherefore it was wisdom in the Lord that we should carry them with us, as we journeyed in the wilderness toward the land of promise. . . . .

"And it came to pass that we did again take our journey in the wilderness, and we did travel nearly eastward from that time forth. And we did travel and wade through much affliction in the wilderness; and our women did bear children in the wilderness. And so great were the blessings of the Lord upon us, that while we did live upon raw meat in the wilderness, our women did give plenty of suck for their children, and were strong, yea, even like unto the men; and they began to bear their journeyings without murmurings. And thus we see that the commandments of God must be fulfilled. And if it so be that the children of men keep the commandments of God, he doth nourish them, and strengthen them, and provide means whereby they can accomplish the things which he hath commanded them; wherefore he did provide means for us while we did sojourn in the wilderness. And we did sojourn for the space of many years, yea, even eight years in the wilderness. And we did come to the land which we called Bountiful, because of its much fruit, and also wild honey; and all these things were prepared of the Lord, that we might not perish. And we beheld the sea, which we called Irreantum, which, being interpreted, is Many waters.

"And it came to pass that we did pitch our tents by the sea-shore; and notwithstanding we had suffered many afflictions and much difficulty, yea, even so much that we cannot write them all, we were exceedingly rejoiced when we came to the sea-shore; and we called the place Bountiful, because of its much fruit. . . . . .

"And it came to pass that the Lord spake unto me, saying: Thou shalt construct a ship after the manner which I shall show thee, that I may carry thy people across these waters. And I saith, Lord, whither shall I go that I may find ore to molten, that I may make tools to construct the ship, after the manner which thou hast shown unto me? And it came to pass that the Lord told me whither I should go to find ore, that I might make tools.

"And it came to pass that I, Nephi, did make bellowses, wherewith to blow the fire, of the skins of beasts; and after that I had made bellowses, that I might have wherewith to blow the fire, I did smite two stones together that I might make fire, for the Lord had not hitherto suffered that we should make much fire, as we journeyed in the wilderness: for he saith, I will make that thy food shall become sweet, that ye cook it not; and I will also be your light in the wilderness; and I will prepare the way before you, if it so be that ye shall keep my commandments; wherefore, inasmuch as ye shall keep my commandments, ye shall be led toward the promised land; and ye shall know that it is by me that ye are led. Yea, and the Lord said also, That after ye have arrived at the promised land, ye shall know that I the Lord am God; and that I the Lord did deliver you from destruction; yea, that I did bring you out of the land of Jerusalem: wherefore I, Nephi, did strive to keep the commandments of the Lord, and I did exhort my brethren to faithfulness and diligence.

"And it came to pass that I did make tools of the ore which I did molten out of the rock. And when my brethren saw that I was about to build a ship, they began to murmur against me, saying: Our brother is a fool, for he thinketh that he can build a ship; yea, and he also thinketh that he can cross these great waters. And thus my brethren did complain against me, and were desirous that they might not labor, for they did not believe that I could build a ship; neither would they believe that I was instructed of the Lord.

"And now it came to pass that I, Nephi, was exceeding sorrowful, because of the hardness of their hearts; and now when they saw that I began to be sorrowful, they were glad in their hearts, insomuch that they did rejoice over me, saying: We knew that ye could not construct a ship, for we knew that ye were lacking in judgment; wherefore, thou canst not accomplish so great a work; and thou art like unto our father, led away by the foolish imaginations of his heart; yea, he hath led us out of the land of Jerusalem, and we have wandered in the wilderness for these many years; and our women have toiled, being big with child; and they have borne children in the wilderness, and suffered all things, save it were death; and it would have been better that they had died before they came out of Jerusalem, than to have suffered these afflictions. Behold, these many years we have suffered in the wilderness, which time we might have enjoyed our possessions and the land of our inheritance; yea, and we might have been happy; and we know that the people which were in the land of Jerusalem were a righteous people, for they kept the statutes and the judgments of the Lord, and all his commandments, according to the law of Moses; wherefore, we know that they are a righteous people; and our father hath judged them, and hath led us away because we would hearken unto his words; yea, and our brother is like unto him. And after this manner of language did my brethren murmur and complain against me.

"And it came to pass that I, Nephi, spake unto them, saying: Do ye believe that our fathers, which were the children of Israel, would have been led away out of the hands of the Egyptians, if they had not hearkened unto the words of the Lord? Yea, do ye suppose that they would have been led out of bondage if the Lord had not commanded Moses that he should lead them out of bondage? Now ye know that the children of Israel were in bondage; and ye know that they were laden with tasks, which were grievous to be borne; wherefore, ye know that it must needs be a good thing for them that they should be brought out of bondage. Now ye know that Moses was commanded of the Lord to do that great work; and ye know that by his word the waters of the Red Sea were divided hither and thither, and they passed through on dry ground. But ye know that the Egyptians were drowned in the Red Sea, which were the armies of Pharaoh; and ye also know that they were fed with manna in the wilderness; yea, and ye also know that Moses, by his word, according to the power of God which was in him, smote the rock, and there came forth water that the children of Israel might quench their thirst; and, notwithstanding, they being led, the Lord their God, their Redeemer, going before them, leading them by day and giving light unto them by night, and doing all things for them which was expedient for man to receive, they hardened their hearts and blinded their minds, and reviled against Moses and against the true and living God.

"And it came to pass that, according to his word, he did lead them; and, according to his word, he did do all things for them; and there was not any thing done save it were by his word. And after they had crossed the river Jordan he did make them mighty, unto the driving out the children of the land; yea, unto the scattering them to destruction. And now do ye suppose that the children of this land, which were in the land of promise, which were driven out by our fathers, do ye suppose that they were righteous? Behold, I say unto you, nay. . . . . . .

"And it came to pass that they did worship the Lord, and did go forth with me; and we did work timbers of curious workmanship. And the Lord did show me from time to time, after what manner I should work the timbers of the ship. Now I, Nephi, did not work the timbers after the manner which was learned by men, neither did I build the ship after the manner of men; but I did build it after the manner which the Lord had shown unto me; wherefore, it was not after the manner of men.

"And I, Nephi, did go into the mount oft, and I did pray oft unto the Lord; wherefore, the Lord showed unto me great things.

"And it came to pass that after I had finished the ship according to the word of the Lord, my brethren beheld that it was good, and that the workmanship thereof was exceeding fine; wherefore, they did humble themselves again before the Lord.

"And it came to pass that the voice of the Lord came unto my father, that we should arise and go down into the ship. And it came to pass that on the morrow, after that we had prepared all things, much fruits and meat from the wilderness, and honey in abundance, and provisions, according to that which the Lord had commanded us, we did go down into the ship with all our loading, and our seeds, and whatsoever thing we had brought with us, every one according to his age; wherefore, we did all go down into the ship with our wives and our children.*

* The Book of Ether gives a further account of eight vessels for other tribes. These vessels, built by the "brother of Jared, according to the instructions of the Lord," are thus described: "They were very light upon the water, even like unto the lightness of a fowl upon the water; and they were built after a manner that they were exceeding tight, even that they would hold water like unto a dish; and the bottom thereof was tight like unto a dish; and the sides thereof were tight like unto a dish; and the ends thereof were peaked; and the top thereof was tight like unto a dish; and the length thereof was the length of a tree." [Breathing-holes, with

"And now my father had begat two sons in the wilderness. The eldest was called Jacob, and the younger Joseph. And it came to pass that after we had all gone down into the ship, and had taken with us our provisions and things which had been commanded us, we did put forth into the sea, and were driven forth before the wind toward the promised land; and after that we had been driven forth before the wind, for the space of many days, behold my brethren and the sons of Ishmael, and also their wives, began to make themselves merry, insomuch that they began to dance and to sing, and to speak with much rudeness, yea, even so that they did forget by what power they had been brought thither; yea, they were lifted up unto exceeding rudeness. And I, Nephi, began to fear exceedingly, lest the Lord should be angry with us, and smite us because of our iniquity, that we should be swallowed up in the depths of the sea; wherefore, I, Nephi, began to speak to them with much soberness; but, behold, they were angry with me, saying: We will not that our younger brother shall be a ruler over us.

"And it came to pass that Laman and Lemuel did take me and bind me with cords, and they did treat

stoppers, were afterward made in the top.] "And the Lord said unto the brother of Jared, Behold ye shall be as a whale in the midst of the sea; nevertheless, I will bring you up again out of the depths of the sea."

me with much harshness; nevertheless, the Lord did suffer it, that he might show forth his power unto the fulfilling of his word which he hath spoken concerning the wicked.

"And it came to pass that after they had bound me, insomuch that I could not move, the compass which had been prepared of the Lord did cease to work; wherefore they knew not whither they should steer the ship, insomuch that there arose a great storm, yea, a great and terrible tempest; and we were driven back upon the waters for the space of three days, and they began to be frightened exceedingly, lest they should be drowned in the sea; nevertheless, they did loose me not. And on the fourth day which we had been driven back the tempest began to be exceeding sore.

"And it came to pass that we were about to be swallowed up in the depths of the sea. And after that we had been driven back upon the waters for the space of four days, my brethren began to see that the judgment of God was upon them, and that they must perish, save that they should repent of their iniquities; wherefore, they came unto me and loosed the bands which were upon my wrists, and behold they had much swollen, exceedingly; and also mine ankles were much swollen, and great was the soreness thereof. Nevertheless, I did look unto my God, and I did praise him all the day long; and I did not murmur against the Lord because of mine afflictions. . . . And it came to pass that after they had loosed me, behold, I took the compass, and it did work whither I desired it. And it came to pass that I prayed unto the Lord; and after that I had prayed, the winds did cease, and the storm did cease, and there was a great calm.

"And it came to pass that I, Nephi, did guide the ship, that we sailed again toward the promised land. And it came to pass that after we had sailed for the space of many days, we did arrive at the promised land; and we went forth upon the land, and did pitch our tents; and we did call it the Promised Land.

"And it came to pass that we did begin to till the earth, and we began to plant seeds; yea, we did put all our seeds into the earth, which we had brought from the land of Jerusalem. And it came to pass that they did grow exceedingly; wherefore we were blessed in abundance.

"And it came to pass that we did find upon the Land of Promise, as we journeyed in the wilderness, that there were beasts in the forests of every kind, both the cow and the ox, and the ass, and the horse, and the goat, and the wild goat, and all manner of wild animals, which were for the use of man. And we did find all manner of ore, both of gold and of silver, and of copper.

"And it came to pass that the Lord commanded me, wherefore I did make plates of ore, that I might engraven upon them the record of my people. And upon the plates which I made I did engraven the record of my father, and also our journeyings in the wilderness, and the prophecies of my father; and also many of mine own prophecies have I engraven upon them. And I knew not at that time when I made them that I should be commanded of the Lord to make these plates; wherefore the record of my father, and the genealogy of his fathers, and the more part of all our proceedings in the wilderness, are engraven upon the plates of which I have spoken. . . . . .

"And after that I had made these plates by way of commandment, I, Nephi, received a commandment that the ministry, and the prophecies, the more plain and precious parts of them, should be written upon these plates; and that the things which were written should be kept for the instruction of my people, which should possess the land, and also for other wise purposes, which purposes are known unto the Lord; wherefore I, Nephi, did make a record upon the other plates, which gives an account, or which gives a greater account of the wars, and contentions, and destruction of my people. And this have I done, and commanded my people that they should do, after that I was gone, and that these plates should be handed down from one generation to another, or from one prophet to another, until further commandments of the Lord. . . . . .

"And thus they did put an end to all those wicked, and secret, and abominable combinations, in the which there was so much wickedness, and so many murders committed. And thus had the twenty-and-second year passed away, and the twenty-and-third year also, and the twenty-and-fourth, and the twenty-and-fifth; and thus had twenty-and-five years passed away, and there had many things transpired which, in the eyes of some, would be great and marvellous; nevertheless, they cannot all be written in this book; yea, this book cannot contain even a hundredth part of what was done among so many people in the space of twenty-and-five years; but behold there are records which do contain all the proceedings of this people, and a more short but true account was given by Nephi; therefore I have made my record of these things according to the record of Nephi, which were engraven on the plates which were called the plates of Nephi. And behold, I do make the record on plates which I have made with mine own hands. And behold, I am called Mormon, being called after the land of Mormon, the land in the which Alma did establish the church among the people; yea, the first church which was established among them after their transgression. Behold, I am a disciple of Jesus Christ, the Son of God. I have been called of him to declare his word among his people, that they might have everlasting life. . . . . .

"And it came to pass in the thirty-and-fourth year, in the first month, in the fourth day of the month, there arose a great storm, such an one as never had been known in all the land; and there was also a great and terrible tempest; and there was terrible thunder, insomuch that it did shake the whole earth as if it was about to divide asunder; and there was exceeding sharp lightnings, such as never had been known in all the land. And the city of Zarahemla did take fire; and the city of Moroni did sink into the depths of the sea, and the inhabitants thereof were drowned; and the earth was carried up upon the city of Moronihah, that in the place of the city thereof there became a great mountain; and there was a great and terrible destruction in the land southward. But behold, there was a more great and terrible destruction in the land northward; for behold, the whole face of the land was changed because of the tempest, and the whirlwinds, and the thunderings, and the lightnings, and the exceeding great quaking of the whole earth; and the highways were broken up, and the level roads were spoiled, and many smooth places became rough, and many great and notable cities were sunk, and many were burned, and many were shook till the buildings thereof had fallen to the earth, and the inhabitants thereof were slain, and the places were left desolate; and there were some cities which remained; but the damage thereof was exceeding great, and there were many in them which were slain; and there were some which were carried away in the whirlwind; and whither they went no man knoweth, save they know that they were carried away; and thus the face of the whole earth became deformed because of the tempests, and the thunderings, and the lightnings, and the quaking of the earth. And behold the rocks were rent in twain; yea, they were broken up upon the face of the whole earth, insomuch that they were found in broken fragments, and in seams, and in cracks, upon all the face of the land. . . . . .

"And it came to pass that there was thick darkness upon the face of all the land, insomuch that the inhabitants thereof which had not fallen could feel the vapor of darkness; and there could be no light because of the darkness, neither candles, neither torches; neither could there be fire kindled with their fine and exceeding dry wood, so that there could not be any light at all; and there was not any light seen, neither fire, nor glimmer, neither the sun, nor the moon, nor the stars, for so great were the mists of darkness which were upon the face of the land.

"And it came to pass that it did last for the space of three days, that there was no light seen; and there was great mourning, and howling, and weeping among all the people continually; yea, great were the groanings of the people, because of the darkness and the great destruction which had come upon them. And in one place they were heard to cry, saying: O that we had repented before this great and terrible day, and had not killed and stoned the prophets, and cast them out; then would our mothers, and our fair daughters, and our children have been spared, and not have been buried up in that great city Moronihah; and thus were the howlings of the people great and terrible. . . . . .

"And now I, Mormon, being about to deliver up the record which I have been making, into the hands of my son Moroni, behold, I have witnessed almost all the destruction of my people, the Nephites. And it is many hundred years after the coming of Christ that I deliver these records into the hands of my son; and it supposeth me that he will witness the entire destruction of my people. But may God grant that he may survive them, that he may write somewhat concerning them, and somewhat concerning Christ, that perhaps some day it may profit them.

"And now I speak somewhat concerning that which I have written, for after that I had made an abridgment from the plates of Nephi down to the reign of this King Benjamin, of which Amaleki spake, I searched among the records which had been delivered into my hands, and I found these plates, which contained this small account of the prophets, from Jacob down to the reign of the King Benjamin; and also many of the words of Nephi. And the things which are upon these plates pleasing me, because of the prophecies of the coming of Christ; and my father's knowing that many of them have been fulfilled; wherefore, I chose these things to finish my record upon them, which remainder of my record I shall take from the plates of Nephi; and I cannot write a hundredth part of the things of my people. But behold, I shall take these plates, which contain these prophesyings and revelations, and put them with the remainder of my record, for they are choice unto me; and I know they will be choice unto my brethren.

"And now I, Mormon, proceed to finish out my record, which I take from the plates of Nephi; and I make it according to the knowledge and the understanding which God hath given me. Wherefore, it came to pass that after Amaleki had delivered up these plates into the hands of King Benjamin, he took them and put them with the other plates which contained records which had been handed down by the kings from generation to generation, until the days of King Benjamin, from generation to generation, until they have fallen into my hands. And I, Mormon, pray to God that they may be preserved from this time henceforth. And I know that they will be preserved; for there are great things written upon them, out of which my people and their brethren shall be judged at the great and last day, according to the word of God which is written. . . . . .

"And now I, Mormon, make a record of the things which I have both seen and heard, and call it the Book of Mormon. And about the time that Ammaron hid up the records unto the Lord, he came unto me, (I being about ten years of age, and I began to be learned somewhat after the manner of the learning of my people,) and Ammaron saith unto me, I perceive that thou art a sober child, and art quick to observe; therefore when ye are about twenty-and-four years old, I would that ye should remember the things that ye have observed concerning this people; and when ye are of that age, go to the land of Antum, unto a hill which shall be called Shim; and there have I deposited unto the Lord all the sacred engravings concerning this people. And behold, ye shall take the plates of Nephi unto yourself, and the remainder shall ye leave in the place where they are; and ye shall engrave upon the plates of Nephi all the things that ye have observed concerning this people. And I, Mormon, being a descendant of Nephi, (and my father's name was Mormon,) I remembered the things which Ammaron commanded me. . . . . .

"And now I finish my record concerning the destruction of my people, the Nephites. And it came to pass that we did march forth before the Lamanites. And I, Mormon, wrote an epistle unto the king of the Lamanites, and desired of him that he would grant unto us that we might gather together our people unto the land of Camorah, by a hill which was called Camorah, and there we would give them battle. . . .

"And it came to pass that when we had gathered in all our people as one to the land of Camorah, behold I, Mormon, began to be old; and knowing it to be the last struggle of my people, and having been commanded of the Lord that I should not suffer that the records which had been handed down by our fathers, which were sacred, to fall into the hands of the Lamanites, (for the Lamanites would destroy them,) therefore I made this record out of the plates of Nephi, and hid up in the hill Camorah all the records which had been intrusted to me by the hand of the Lord, save it were these few plates which I gave unto my son Moroni.* . . . . .

"Behold I, Moroni, do finish the record of my father Mormon. Behold, I have but few things to

* From the Book of Ether: "And behold these two stones will I give unto thee, and ye shall seal them up also, with the things which ye shall write. For behold the language which ye shall write I have confounded; wherefore, I will cause in my own due time that these stones shall magnify to the eyes of men those things which ye shall write." [Urim and Thummim.]

write, which things I have been commanded of my father. And now it came to pass that after the great and tremendous battle at Camorah, behold, the Nephites which had escaped into the country southward, were hunted by the Lamanites until they were all destroyed; and my father also was killed by them; and I, even I remaineth alone to write the sad tale of the destruction of my people. But behold they are gone, and I fulfil the commandment of my father. Behold, four hundred years have passed away since the coming of our Lord and Saviour. And behold, the Lamanites have hunted my people, the Nephites, down from city to city, and from place to place, even until they are no more; and great has been their fall; yea, great and marvellous is the destruction of my people, the Nephites. . . . . .

"Behold, I am Moroni; and were it possible, I would make all things known unto you. Behold, I make an end of speaking concerning this people. I am the son of Mormon, and my father was a descendant of Nephi; and I am the same which hideth up this record unto the Lord; the plates thereof are of no worth, because of the commandment of the Lord. For he truly saith, That no one shall have them to get gain; but the record thereof is of great worth; and whoso shall bring it to light, him will the Lord bless. For none can have power to bring it to light, save it be given him of God; for God will that it shall be done with an eye single to his glory, or the welfare of the ancient and long-dispersed covenant people of the Lord. And blessed be him that shall bring this thing to light; for it shall be brought out of darkness unto light, according to the word of God; yea, it shall be brought out of the earth, and it shall shine forth out of darkness and come unto the knowledge of the people: and it shall be done by the power of God; and if there be faults, they be the faults of a man."

CHAPTER IX.

Origin of the Book of Mormon—Who wrote it?—Mormon Legends—Solomon Spaulding's Fable—Rigdon and Smith the Schemers.

The Book of Mormon, viewed in any sense as a literary production, is scarcely worthy of criticism or remark; but when considered "as the accepted groundwork of the religious faith of a people whose growth has been most extraordinary, and whose fanaticism is an astonishing phenomenon in psychology, the book has more than an ephemeral interest" for the student of human philosophy. As a curiosity merely, not as a readable romance, it commands a place in respectable libraries.

But neither the specimen passages reprinted in the preceding pages, nor the book in its entirety, furnish any satisfactory answer to the question of its origin and purpose. Nor is such answer found in the fabulous visions and revelations of the pretender Smith, nominally corroborated as they are by the testimony of his eleven confederate witnesses. The glyph problem, even if Smith had obtained one of those fossil curiosities, as has been suggested in another connection, can in no wise apply in this case. These questions, therefore, must necessarily be left to individual choice of solution, as between the conflicting theories and evidence at hand; and it will best accord with the design of this publication, to present for that choice the opposing conclusions of Mormons and Gentiles.

"That a single man, in the midst of the enlightenment of this century, should have been able to throw the lines of mysticism so thoroughly over the minds of hundreds and thousands of men and women, is not more wonderful than the earnest and self-denying faith with which his devotees have sustained an unbroken unity, under circumstances of remarkable privation and peril. Nor is it less surprising that the assumption of a power very nearly absolute, by one man, who is regarded as the legitimate successor of the original prophet, has come to be accepted by this people as a divine ordination, and that to one guiding spirit alone is yielded the homage and obedience which insure the autocratic sway of Brigham Young. Considered in all their relations—religious, political, moral, or social—the Mormons are a curious people. Occupying for their headquarters a portion of the American continent which is far removed from the influences of civilization,* and indeed is for many months in the

* This description (from Introduction to Wright & Co.'s New York edition "Book of Mormon") dates back to the beginning of the Mor-

year totally inaccessible—cooped up among overhanging mountains—destitute of the refinements of ordinary social life—bent beneath the sway of an unscrupulous hierarchy—holding to practices which, elsewhere than in their own territory, would subject them to the penalties of the law; and, withal, noted for a spirit of zeal, industry, and perseverance, which has enabled them to convert the wildest moods of Nature into servants of their will—the Mormons have earned an enduring reputation for sincerity, and energy, and capacity. When the secrets of their *origin*, and progress and government, shall have been added to the published record of their religious belief, this people will rank among the most extraordinary of all the sects that have sprung into life as the world has run its course."

First, in the pursuit of information showing the true origin and correct history of the Book of Mormon, let the reader consider the legendary account adopted by the Mormons themselves. This is furnished in a published statement by Parley P. Pratt, the early convert at Palmyra, and the contemporary of Smith and Rigdon at their first confederated appearance in Ohio, and also an accepted oracle in the subsequent history of Mormonism. According to that authority, the Latter-Day Saints claim that "a portion

mon colony in Utah, when that territory was yet in the wilds of Mexico, and before its acquisition by the United States.

of their history runs back to that extremely remote age when the tongues were confounded at the Tower of Babel. They hold that at the time of that event, the tribes of the earth were scattered abroad, and that the migrations of one particular colony were especially directed by the Lord, who led the favored few across the sea to the Western Continent, now called America. This colony inhabited America for some fifteen hundred years, but were destroyed for their wickedness at a period about six hundred years before Christ. A prophet, Ether, was their historian, and one of the books in the Mormon Bible, which bears his name, gives a full account of his genealogy and of the nature of his prophetic office. Ether seems to have been a lineal descendant from Jared, and Jared was one of the favored colony, led out from the polyglot tribulation at the Tower, and conducted subsequently to the land of rest which was provided on the territory now known as America. The prophet lived to see the last vestige of his nation become extinct, and, having finished his record of its history and destruction, deposited it, under divine direction, in the locality where it was found by another colony.

"The second colony, according to the best Mormon authority, was composed of Israelites, and came from Jerusalem about the year 600 B. C., occupying the place of the original colony, which was then extinct, and repeopling America. The new colonists were descendants of the tribe of Joseph. They grew and multiplied, became rich and powerful, and in process of time divided into two nations; one of which, the Nephites, so named after its founder Nephi, became noted for enlightenment and civilization,—while the other branch, the Lamanites, taking their name from their leader Laman, lapsed into barbarism, and were destitute of the refinements and advantages which attend a state of civilized existence. The Mormon historians make this latter branch the immediate progenitors of the American Indians.

"The Mormon history proceeds to record the progress of the opposing nations of the Nephites and the Lamanites. The Nephites appear to have been highly favored of the Lord. They enjoyed visions, received the visitation of angels, and the gift of prophecy was handed down from age to age. Finally, they were blessed with a personal appearance of Jesus Christ after His resurrection from the dead; received from Him the doctrine of the Gospel, and were invested with the power of foretelling the events of the future. In this happy condition of grace and wisdom, the race of the Nephites continued until the fourth century of the Christian era, when, through temptation, they fell from their high estate, and finally were destroyed by their wicked neighbors, the Lamanites. The most noted prophet of the golden age of the Nephites was *Mormon.* By divine commandment, Mormon made an abridgment of the sacred records, which contained the history of his forefathers, narrated the prophecies which were made to them, and sketched the events which attended the introduction of the Gospel among them. The history of his own time was appended to this record, and Mormon put the finishing touch to his historical labors, by narrating the destruction of his nation—both he and his predecessor Ether having been permitted to escape the general destruction, in order that the record of the great events which produced the catastrophe might descend safely to future generations. Mormon, having completed his work, laid him down to die, and intrusted to his son Moroni the task of concealing the plates upon which he had recorded the story of his nation. From this point commences the history of the Mormon Bible.

"In order to preserve the plates from falling into the impious hands of the Lamanites, Moroni deposited them carefully in the earth, in a locality then called the Hill Camorah—now a part of Ontario County, in the State of New York. The record was carefully sealed up, and buried several feet below the surface of the hill, and the date of that occurrence is fixed about A. D. 420. Fourteen hundred years passed away, until, on the 22d day of September, 1827, an angel of the Lord directed Joseph Smith, Jr. (the original prophet), to exhume the long-buried history."*

The legend proceeds with descriptions of the metallic volume, a part of which was sealed and not to be seen, even by Smith himself, until further revelation, and also of the Urim and Thummim or large spectacles to be used in translating, which are substantially the same as given elsewhere.

According to similar "latter-day" accounts, the wonderful event was followed by great popular commotion; though these things were not perceived or heard of at the time and locality of the original story. The following exciting description has been published by the Mormons:

"Soon the news of these discoveries by Joseph Smith, Jr., spread abroad throughout all those parts. False reports, misrepresentations, and base slanders, flew as if upon the wings of the wind, in every direction. His house was frequently beset by mobs and evil-designing persons. Several times he was shot at, and very narrowly escaped. Every device was used to get the plates away from him. And being continually in danger of his life from a gang of abandoned wretches, he at length concluded to leave the place and go to Pennsylvania; and, accordingly, packed up his goods, putting the plates into a barrel

* Mormon publication in London, 1854, by Parley P. Pratt. Then a foreign missionary in the cause of the "saints."

of beans, and proceeded upon his journey. He had not gone far, before he was overtaken by an officer with a search-warrant, who flattered himself with the idea that he should surely obtain the plates; but after searching very diligently, he was sadly disappointed at not finding them. Mr. Smith then drove on, but before he got to his journey's end he was again overtaken by the officer on the same business, and after ransacking the wagon very carefully, he went his way as much chagrined as in the first instance, at not being able to discover the object of his search. Without any further molestation, he pursued his journey until he came into the northern part of Pennsylvania, near the Susquehanna River. Here, by the power of God, and with the aid of two crystals set in a bow (the Urim and Thummim), he translated the unsealed portion of the records into the English tongue, in obedience to the divine command."

The latter portion of this Mormon second-thought—the alleged procurement of the "translations" in Pennsylvania—is probably a little nearer the truth than the pretensions first put forth by Smith, Cowdery, Harris, and their prime associates; for their story then was, that the translations were made in the manner before stated, at Smith's residence in Manchester. Whereas, no doubt, the exact truth is, that a *copy* of their production was made from a manuscript then held by an accomplice in Pennsylvania.

The whole idea of an attempt to harm Smith in any way, or to rob him of his "golden bible," is purely a Mormon invention, based upon no other circumstance in truth, than that an individual creditor in vain sent a constable after him in the hope of securing the payment of a small debt.

"Elder Oliver Cowdery," who was one of the pioneer Mormons at Manchester and Palmyra, published at Independence, Mo., in 1834, a description of the hill where Smith claimed to have obtained the records, with the following ingenious account of their deposit by Moroni; and the same account was republished by one of the Mormon missionaries at Edinburgh in 1840:

"How far below the surface these records were placed by Moroni, I am unable to say; but from the fact that they had been some fourteen hundred years buried, and that, too, on the side of a hill so steep, one is ready to conclude that they were some feet below, as the earth would naturally wear, more or less, in that length of time; but they being placed toward the top of the hill, the ground would not remove as much as at two-thirds of the way up, perhaps. Another circumstance would prevent a wearing of the earth; in all probability, as soon as timber had time to grow, the hill was covered after the Nephites were destroyed, and the roots of the same would hold the surface; however, on this point, I shall leave every man to draw his own conclusion, and form his own speculation. A hole of sufficient depth was dug; at the bottom of this was laid a stone of suitable size, the upper surface being smooth; at each edge was placed a large quantity of cement, and into this cement at the four edges of this stone, were placed erect four others; their bottom edges resting in the cement, at the outer edges of the first stone. The four last named, when placed erect, formed a box; the corners, or where the edges of the four came in contact, were also cemented so firmly, that the moisture from without was prevented from entering. It is to be observed, also, that the inner surface of the four erect or side stones was smooth. This box was sufficiently large to admit a breast-plate, such as was used by the ancients to defend the chest, etc., from the arrows and weapons of their enemy. From the bottom of the box, or from the breast-plate, arose three small pillars, composed of the same description of cement used on the edges; and upon these three pillars was placed the record. This box containing the record was covered with another stone, the bottom surface being flat, and the upper crowning."

Does the reader require proof of the utter untruth of all this parade of particulars about finding any thing of the kind pretended, either in Ontario County or elsewhere? But it is a noticeable incident in the whole progress of the imposture, that the uneducated and ignorant character of Smith was turned to his advantage over his followers. His want of cultivation in respect to "the world's wisdom," precluded in their minds the idea of the exercise of any natural or acquired faculties in producing his wonderful revelations and translations. Their reasoning was: "He is unlearned of men, therefore how could he acquire the ancient learning displayed, if it were not supernaturally communicated to him?" And they argued, that he could not have made the translations without the plates. Convincing logic for the Mormon fanatics!

Here comes in for application and reflection the coincidence of Sidney Rigdon's long-continued incognito sojournments at the money-digger's residence during the Mormon incubation. Who can doubt that he and Smith had become confederates in a grand scheme of cupidity and imposture? They had surreptitiously possessed themselves of a fabulous composition peculiarly adapted to their design. Secrecy and falsehood were necessary to the success of such a scheme, and to these, it is self-evident, they were mutually sworn. The following explanatory statements, received from the best authority, supply the proof:

"About the year 1809, the Reverend Solomon Spaulding, a clergyman who had graduated from Dartmouth College, and settled in the town of Cherry Valley, in the State of New York, removed from that place to New Salem (Conneaut), Ashtabula County, Ohio. Mr. Spaulding was an enthusiastic archæologist. The region to which he removed was rich in American antiquities. The mounds and traces of fortifications abounding there, which have puzzled the brains of many patient explorers, attracted his attention. On account of failing health, he had retired from the active labors of his profession; and being possessed of a lively imagination, and familiar with the classics and ancient history, he sought to beguile the hours of retirement and employ his mind by writing a fabulous historical record of a long-lost race, adopting the hypothesis that his manuscript was found in one of the mounds. He accepted the theory that the American continent had been peopled by a colony of the ancient Israelites. The ample material by which he was surrounded, full of mythical interest and legendary suggestiveness, led him to the conception of the curious literary project referred to. The work was commenced, and progressed slowly for some time. Portions of it were read by Mr. Spaulding to his friends, as its different sections were completed, and after about three years' labor, that is, in 1812 or 1813, the volume was completed, bearing the title of 'The Manuscript Found.'" Mr. Spaulding submitted his work to a printer named Patterson, at Pittsburg, Pa., with a view to its publication on joint account. The printing proposal, however, for some reason, was not carried out, and the manuscript remained in Patterson's office until 1816, when it was reclaimed by the author, who in that year removed to Amity, Washington County, N. Y., where he died in 1827. The manuscript remained in the widow's possession until it was missed or stolen from a trunk in Otsego County, where she had removed, about the time the "Book of Mormon" began to be publicly mentioned.

"In the employment of the printer Patterson was a versatile genius, one Sidney Rigdon, to whom no trade came amiss, and who happened at the time to be a journeyman printer at work with Patterson. Disputations on questions of theology were the peculiar delight of Rigdon; and the probable solution of the mystery of this Book of Mormon, is found in the fact, that he had made a copy of Spaulding's manuscript, and communicated information of the existence of the fictitious record to Joseph Smith, Jr.," after becoming acquainted with Smith's money-digging operations. Patterson died in 1826.

From all the evidence possessed, there can be no doubt that the plan of founding a new system of religion was concocted by these two shrewd and unscrupulous persons, and that the Spaulding fable was its basis. "The fact that the style of the Mormon book so closely imitates that of the received version of the Bible—a point which seems to have been constantly kept in view by Mr. Spaulding, probably in order to invest the fiction with a stronger character of reality—answered admirably for the purposes of Rigdon and Smith. Superstition readily embraces any thing which has a show of reality, especially if it be sustained by a sanction apparently divine; and the success of this remarkable literary imposture is not more wonderful than the devotion of the Mohammedan to the Koran, which, like the Book of Mormon, is accepted as the standard of a religious faith. The Millerite fanaticism was less marked, but found not less earnest followers."

These statements are derived from the declarations of Mrs. Spaulding herself, as made in 1831, and subsequently. In that year, Dr. Philastus Hurlburt, living near New Salem, Ohio (after Mormonism had become seated in that State), who had obtained a copy of the Book of Mormon, came by appointment of a public meeting of his neighbors, in pursuit of information on the subject, to Palmyra, N. Y., where he stated that he was acquainted with several reliable persons who had seen the Spaulding manuscript, and who recognized its identity in the main with the printed book. He furthermore obtained the same recognition from Mrs. Spaulding, and from Mr. John Spaulding, a brother of the deceased.

No doubt the Spaulding manuscript was altered by Rigdon and Smith to suit the case in hand and meet rising exigencies. Indeed, it is apparent from the marked changes in style of composition occurring in numbers of instances, that emendations and additions were made by some other than the original writer's hand. Then, too, the verbose title-page—the "preface" in regard to the translations lost by the incendiarism of Mrs. Harris—the testimonies of witnesses, and the long line of revelations that followed—which are not presumed to have been composed by the illiterate Smith, but by Rigdon during Smith's lifetime—all these are strong corroborative considerations connected with the proofs that Rigdon supplied the literary aliment needed in conforming the Spaulding production to the grand copartnership Mormon speculation. And it is not known that he has ever disclaimed the part that for more than thirty years has been publicly assigned to him in the great plagiarism and imposture.

Rigdon was in possession of a copy of this manuscript before he had heard of Smith's money-digging delusions, and the application ultimately made of it, as Smith's accomplice, was incidental. Is it not a noteworthy retribution in his case, that his Mormon history should come to a sudden close soon after the murder of Joseph Smith and his brother Hyrum in 1844, when he was defeated by Brigham Young in a contest for the successorship as prophet, and quit Nauvoo and the "saints," under the ban of expulsion? He was expelled from a church and colony which he had been so instrumental in bringing into being, and went to Allegany County, N. Y., where he has lived to the present time. A citizen of that county, in reply to inquiries, writes: "Rigdon used to lecture on various scientific subjects, and was regarded as a man of ability and a good public speaker. He has been solicited to publish an authentic history of the Mormon speculation, but is said to decline doing so from fear of Mormon vengeance. It is supposed he might, if so minded, give a better reason for his refusal. He is now seventy-five years of age, and his habits are those of seclusion and reticence."

In the pursuit of data for this history, the favor of information was sought from Mr. Rigdon. Preliminary to a proposed personal interview, a note was addressed to him by mail, at "Friendship, Allegany County, N. Y.," of which the following is a copy:

[Prepaid and post-stamps enclosed.]

PALMYRA, N. Y., *April* 19, 1867.

Mr. SIDNEY RIGDON, *Friendship, Allegany County, N. Y.*

DEAR SIR: I am emboldened to address you, without the benefit of a personal acquaintance that you will recognize, from having received a personal introduction to you here in 1830. I heard your sermon at the hall of our Palmyra Young Men's Association in that year, in reference to the then new Mormon revelation according to Joseph Smith, Jr.

Are you willing to be consulted personally regarding the origin of the Book of Mormon? Or, will you favor me by mail with any information such as may suggest itself to you as useful to me in carrying out a design in hand to write up for publication, a brief, connected, and truthful history of Mormonism and its founders, from the commencement to the present date of that system?

I was acquainted with Joseph Smith, Jr., and with his father and the family, during their residence in Palmyra and Manchester.

I shall feel obliged, at any rate, for an intimation of your views and disposition in this matter, at your early convenience, and would be happy to reciprocate your kindness.

Very respectfully,

POMEROY TUCKER.

No answer has been received from Mr. Rigdon.

Brigham Young, now the autocrat-prophet of the saints at Salt Lake City, in reply to the admonition of a friend at the time he joined Smith and the Mormons at Kirtland, said: "The doctrine Smith teaches is all I know about the matter; bring any thing against that if you can; as to any thing else, I don't care if he acts like a devil; he has brought forth a religion that will save us, if we abide by it; he may get drunk every day of his life, sleep with his neighbor's wife every night, gamble, and run horses, and be guilty of all you allege against him—I don't care any thing about these questions, for I don't embrace the *man* in my faith." This closed the argument.

Peter Ingersoll, a respectable citizen of Palmyra, who had believingly taken some part in Smith's money-digging operations, and was at first inclined to put faith in his "Golden Bible" pretension, declared under oath, that "Smith told him the whole story was a hoax; that he had found no such book; but that as he had got the d—d fools fixed, he was bound to carry out the fun."

Testimony of the same tenor on this head might be multiplied, if it were not considered superfluous.

CHAPTER X.

Kirtland, Ohio—Maturity of the Mormon Church—Theology of the Saints—Brigham Young converted—Martin Harris in Council—A Division of the Mormons remove to Missouri—Saints under Proscription.

At Kirtland, Ohio, the Mormons had a successful though brief experience in the outset of their organization which had been imperfectly effected at their starting-place in Manchester, N. Y. The nucleus of their Church and hierarchy may be said to have advanced to maturity at this point in their progress. Their doctrines, at first not at all clearly defined, were yet somewhat vague and contradictory. It is presumed that neither Smith nor Rigdon had at this time determined what should be their precise character. The new religion needed its finishing touch, but the "revelation" capital was ample for this object. Aided as they were by Parley P. Pratt, whose remarkable instantaneous conversion had occurred at Manchester, all confusion and conflict in regard to the fundamental creed were speedily dispelled before the light of the Mormon gospel.

Joseph Smith, Sr., the first "patriarch and president" of the Church, soon removed with his family to Kirtland, and fulfilled the dignity of his office. Harris early made a purchase of property there, and took his place in the Church with the Smiths, Rigdon, Pratt, Cowdery, the Whitmers, and other pioneers—making occasional return visits in looking after his property affairs at Palmyra.

The next interest was to disseminate to the people the newly revealed "latter-day" religion. The system of missionary labor already inaugurated at Mentor, was put in active requisition; the emissaries pressed the cause with zeal and artistic effect; the trumpet of "the true gospel" was sounded to the gentiles; the superstitious and ignorant were captivated; respectable men and women quaked amid the scene; and conversions were multiplied and blazoned abroad. A sensation was produced unparalleled in the annals of that community; and multitudes, embracing the Smith and Rigdon theory, rushed into the new Zion, as if believing the last days were at hand in sober verity. And fanaticism stood aghast!

Thus was the Mormon Church matured, and the colony of the saints speedily enlarged. Incomers from a distance, professing the faith, reënforced their numbers, including some families of character, influence, and wealth. The prophet, though "uneducated and unlearned in worldly wisdom (quoting the phrase used), was acknowledged to possess by the spirit of revelation great heavenly gifts, such as "speaking in unknown tongues, performing miracles, and healing the sick."

No doubt Rigdon from the start had more to do with this strange adventure than Smith; for without the fictitious "records" derived through his instrumentality from the Spaulding fable, the Mormon device, in all probability, would never have been invented. But as the result of circumstances, Smith was necessarily the nominal chief; and, considering his lack of cultivation, he must have been naturally the superior genius of the two. He had been put forward as the prophet, seer, and revelator, and his native sagacity was equal to his opportunity. He availed himself of his advantage in maintaining his preëminence as the grand oracle and generalissimo; and he continued to exercise this superiority until the day of his death.

Finding himself surrounded and sustained by large and increasing numbers of believing followers, including some people of ample pecuniary means, Smith tried a bold venture upon their credulity in his own behalf. This was a "revelation" which he communicated to his disciples, to the effect that they should "immediately build a house for the prophet, in which he might live and translate." It was in February, 1831, and the command was cheerfully accepted and obeyed. Another revelation, alike successful, shortly followed, commanding that "my chosen Joseph shall not labor for a living."

Though the impostor "seemed to intelligent men little better than a buffoon, his followers regarded him as almost deserving of adoration," and he was enabled by their tribute to revel in whatever luxury or profligacy was most agreeable to his vulgar taste and ambition. His power was now next to omnipotent in Mormondom.

Brigham Young was converted and joined the Mormons at Kirtland in 1832. Like Joseph Smith, Jr., he was a native of Vermont, being his senior by four years. It is a further noteworthy coincidence, that all his father's family, consisting of five sons with himself, and six daughters, became Mormons — the father, John Young, afterward becoming president and patriarch of the Church. Furthermore, Brigham's peculiarities of character were similar to Joseph's. He was shrewd, bold, and resolute, possessing an almost intuitive knowledge of men. He soon attracted attention, and became influential with his brethren. They were involuntarily swayed by his strong, electrical will; and he was recognized as a man born to rule and lead the masses. He was soon ordained one of the quorum of Twelve Apostles that had been organized; and in 1836, the president of that body having apostatized, he was elected to suc-

BRIGHAM YOUNG.

ceed him. He went forth and preached and proselyted with marked success. From that day to this his influence and power within the jurisdiction of Mormondom has been resistless.

Brigham Young was early trained to farming, which was his father's occupation, but had learned the trade of painter and glazier, which he followed in the State of New York, until his Mormon conversion at Kirtland. Here the coincidence between him and Smith is broken, for the latter never learned a trade, nor harbored a disposition to "labor for a living."

Up to 1834, the Mormon creed and system of church government were altogether subject to the caprices of "revelation." Smith, sustained by Rigdon, Pratt, and Young, was the supreme ruler in fact over both the spiritual and temporal affairs of his disciples. It became necessary, to avoid possible discontents and jealousies, to have an outward form of organization. In carrying out this purpose a high council was formed as follows:

"This day a general council of twenty-four high priests assembled at the house of Joseph Smith, Jr., by revelation, and proceeded to organize the high council of the Church of Christ, which was to consist of twelve high-priests, and one or three presidents, as the case might require. The high council was appointed by revelation for the purpose of settling important difficulties which might arise in the Church, which could not be settled by the Church or the bishop's council to the satisfaction of the parties.—"Joseph Smith, Jr., Sidney Rigdon, and Frederick G. Williams, were acknowledged presidents by the voice of the council; and Joseph Smith, Sr., John Smith, Joseph Coe, John Johnson, Martin Harris, John S. Carter, Jared Carter, Oliver Cowdery, Samuel H. Smith, Orson Hyde, Sylvester Smith, and Luke Johnson, high-priests, were chosen to be a standing council for the Church, by the unanimous voice of the council."

Each quorum has its president; and the president of the quorum of three is the president of the high council, and over all the Church, from whom "comes the administration of ordinances and blessings upon the Church, by the laying on of hands." Joseph Smith, Jr., was the first president. The president is "the seer, revelator, and prophet, having all the gifts of God, which he bestows upon the head of the Church." As president of the high council, he may, "in cases of difficulty respecting doctrine or principle, inquire and obtain the mind of the Lord by revelation."

The prophet had previously provided for his supremacy in the revelation:

"Behold, there shall be a record kept among you, and in it thou shalt be called a seer, a translator, a prophet, an apostle of Jesus Christ, an elder of the

Church, through the will of God the Father, and the grace of our Lord Jesus Christ, being inspired of the Holy Ghost to lay the foundation thereof, and to build it up unto the most holy faith."

And the following important celestial enunciation was added:

"But behold, verily, verily, I say unto thee, no one shall be appointed to receive commandments and revelations in this Church excepting my servant Joseph Smith, Jr., for he receiveth them even as Moses; and thou shalt be obedient unto the things which I shall give unto him, even as Aaron, to declare faithfully the commandments and revelations with power and authority unto the Church. And if thou art led at any time by the Comforter to speak or teach, or at all times by the way of commandment unto the Church, thou mayest do it; but thou shalt not write by way of commandment, but by wisdom. And thou shalt not command him who is at thy head, and at the head of the Church; for I have given him the keys of the mysteries and the revelations which are sealed, until I shall appoint unto them another in his stead."

By these exalted authorities, the prophet becomes the president of the Church, and preserves his absolute power over Mormondom. This absolutism was exercised in continuing to put forth revelations, "performing miracles, preaching in unknown tongues, healing the sick," and sending off missionaries; and at the same time securing to himself nearly all the wealth of his followers, under a system of tithing and other forms of ecclesiastical appropriation.

Tithing, in the Mormon hierarchy, is a regular system of the appropriation of individual property for the support and aggrandizement of the prophet and his priesthood. By an early revelation Smith discovered that those having property should convey it to the bishop and his counsellors for the support of the poor, for the purchase of lands for the public benefit of the Church, and the building of houses of worship, etc. In August it was revealed to Smith that "all the moneys which can be spared, it mattereth not whether it be little or much, be sent up unto the land of Zion, unto them whom I have appointed to receive."

Subsequently, to meet the rising emergencies, the prophet gave out this very definite revelation:

"In answer to the question, O Lord, show unto thy servants how much thou requirest of the properties for a tithing? Verily, thus saith the Lord, I require all their surplus property to be put into the hands of the bishop of my Church of Zion, for the building of mine house, and for the laying the foundation of Zion, and for the priesthood, and for the debts of the presidency of my Church; and this shall be the beginning of the yearly tithing of my people; and after that, those who have been thus tithed shall pay one-tenth of all their interest annually, and this shall be a standing law unto them forever, for my holy priesthood, saith the Lord. Verily, I say unto you, it shall come to pass that all those who gather unto the land of Zion shall be tithed of their surplus properties, and shall observe this law, or they shall not be found worthy to abide among you."

The machinery of church government is diversified in its functions, and is not altogether apparent to the profane. The great, studied design, has been to secure despotic power in the few chief impostors, and thus perpetuate the Mormon hierarchy.

There are two priesthoods in the Church—the Melchisedek and the Aaronic (which latter includes the Levitical). All other authorities are appendages to one or the other of these priesthoods. Each priesthood holds the key of the peculiar mysteries which it has in charge. The *key* is an important emblem in Mormon symbolics. All heavenly mysteries are duly locked up, and cannot be opened except by the agent who is authorized to hold and use the key. The Melchisedek is the superior priesthood, and consists of high-priests and elders; the Aaronic is inferior, and made up of bishops, priests, teachers, and deacons. The Melchisedek priesthood is clustered about with holy sanctions and sublime mysteries, which strike awe into the minds of the simple-minded believers. For instance:

"And the sons of Moses, according to the holy

priesthood which he received under the hand of his father-in-law Jethro, and Jethro received it under the hand of Caleb, and Caleb received it under the hand of Elihu, and Elihu under the hand of Jeremy, and Jeremy under the hand of God, and God under the hand of Esaias, and Esaias received it under the hand of God; Esaias also lived in the days of Abraham, and was blessed of him; which Abraham received the priesthood from Melchisedek, who received it through the lineage of his fathers, even till Noah; and from Noah till Enoch, through the lineage of their fathers; and from Enoch to Abel, who was slain by the conspiracy of his brother, who received the priesthood by the commandments of God, by the hand of his father Adam, who was the first man; which priesthood continueth in the Church of God in all generations, and is without beginning of days or end of years."

The power and authority of the Melchisedek priesthood is to hold the keys of all the spiritual blessings of the Church, to have the privilege of receiving the mysteries of the kingdom of heaven, to have the heavens opened unto them, and to enjoy the communion and presence of God the Father, and Jesus Christ the Mediator of the new covenant.

The power and authority of the lesser, or Aaronic priesthood, is to hold the keys of the ministering of angels, and to administer in outward ordinances—the letter of the gospel—the baptism of repentance for the remission of sins, agreeably to the covenants and commandments.*

The following sketch of the "Faith and Doctrine of the Mormon Church" has been publicly put forth as the accepted theology of Mormonism:

"First, we believe in God the Eternal Father, and in his Son Jesus Christ, and in the Holy Ghost, who bears record of them, the same throughout all ages and forever.

"We believe that all mankind, by the transgression of their first parents, and not by their own sins, were brought under the curse and penalty of that transgression which consigned them to an eternal banishment from the presence of God, and their bodies to an endless sleep in the dust, never more to rise, and their spirits to endless misery under the power of Satan; and that, in this awful condition, they were utterly lost, and fallen, and had no power of their own to extricate themselves therefrom.

"We believe that through the sufferings, death, and atonement of Jesus Christ, all mankind, without one exception, are to be completely and fully redeemed, both body and spirit, from the endless banishment and curse to which they were consigned by Adam's transgression, and that this universal salvation and redemption of the whole human family from the endless penalty of the original sin, is effected

* Ferris's "Utah and the Mormons."

without any conditions whatsoever on their part; that is, that they are not required to believe, or repent, or be baptized, or do any thing else, in order to be redeemed from that penalty; for whether they believe or disbelieve, whether they repent or remain impenitent, whether they are baptized or unbaptized, whether they keep the commandments or break them, whether they are righteous or unrighteous, it will make no difference in relation to their redemption, both spirit and body, from the penalty of Adam's transgression. The most righteous man that ever lived on the earth, and the most wicked wretch of the whole human family, were both placed under the same curse, without any transgression or agency of their own, and they both alike will be redeemed from that curse without any agency or conditions on their part. Paul says, Rom. v. 18: 'Therefore, as by the offence of one, judgment came upon all men to condemnation; even so, by the righteousness of one, the free gift came upon all men unto the justification of life.' This is the reason why all men are redeemed from the grave. This is the reason that the spirits of all men are restored to their bodies. This is the reason that all men are redeemed from their first banishment and restored into the presence of God; and this is the reason that the Saviour said, John xii. 32, 'If I be lifted up from the earth, I will draw all men unto me.' After this full, complete, and universal redemption, restoration, and salvation of the whole of Adam's race, through the atonement of Jesus Christ, without faith, repentance, baptism, or any other works, then all and every one of them will enjoy eternal life and happiness, never more to be banished from the presence of God if they themselves have committed no sin: for the penalty of the original sin can have no more power over them at all, for Jesus hath destroyed its power, broken the bands of the first death, obtained the victory over the grave, delivered all its captives, and restored them from their first banishment into the presence of his Father; hence eternal life will be theirs, if they themselves are not found transgressors of some law.

"We believe that all mankind, in their infant state, are incapable of knowing good and evil, and of obeying or disobeying a law; and that therefore there is no law given to them, and that where there is no law there is no transgression; hence they are innocent, and if they should all die in their infant state, they would enjoy eternal life, not being transgressors themselves, neither accountable for Adam's sin.

"We believe that all mankind, in consequence of the fall, after they grow up from their infant state, and come to the years of understanding, know good and evil, and are capable of obeying and disobeying a law, and that a law is given against doing evil; and that the penalty affixed is a second banishment from the presence of God, both body and spirit, after they have been redeemed from the first banishment and restored into his presence.

"We believe that the penalty of this second law can have no effect upon persons who have not had the privilege, in this life, of becoming acquainted therewith; for although the light that is in them teaches them good and evil, yet that light does not teach them the law against doing evil, nor the penalty thereof.

"We believe that all who have done evil, having a knowledge of the law, or afterward, in this life, coming to the knowledge thereof, are under its penalty, which is not inflicted in this world, but in the world to come. Therefore such, in this world, are prisoners, shut up under the sentence of the law, awaiting, with awful fear, for the time of judgment, when the penalty shall be inflicted, consigning them to a second banishment from the presence of their Redeemer, who had redeemed them from the penalty of the first law. Be assured, O sinner, that thou canst not devise any way of thine own to escape, nor do any thing that will atone for thy sins. Therefore thy case is hopeless, unless God has devised some way for thy deliverance; but do not let despair seize upon thee; for though thou art under the sentence of a broken law, and hast no power to atone for thy sins, and redeem thyself therefrom, yet there is hope in thy case, for He who gave the law has devised a way for thy deliverance. That same Jesus, who hath atoned for the original sin, and will redeem all mankind from the penalty thereof, hath also atoned for thy sins, and offereth salvation and deliverance to thee, on certain conditions to be complied with on thy part.

"We believe that the first condition to be complied with on the part of sinners is, to believe in God, and in the sufferings and death of his Son Jesus Christ to atone for the sins of the whole world, and in his resurrection and ascension on high, to appear in the presence of his Father, to make intercession for the children of men, and in the Holy Ghost, which is given to all who obey the gospel.

"That the second condition is, to repent: that is, all who believe, according to the first condition, are required to come humbly before God, and confess their sins with a broken heart and contrite spirit, and turn away from them, and cease from all their evil deeds, and make restitution to all whom they have in any way injured, as far as it is in their power.

"That the third condition is, to be baptized by immersion in water in the name of the Father, Son, and Holy Ghost, for remission of sins: and that this ordinance is to be administered by one who is called and authorized of Jesus Christ to baptize, otherwise it is illegal, and of no advantage, and not accepted by him; and that it is to be administered only to those persons who believe and repent, according to the two preceding conditions.

"And that the fourth condition is, to receive the laying on of hands, in the name of Jesus Christ, for the gift of the Holy Ghost: and that this ordinance is to be administered by the apostles or elders, whom the Lord Jesus hath called and authorized to lay on hands, otherwise it is of no advantage, being illegal in the sight of God; and that it is to be administered only to those persons who believe, repent, and are baptized into this Church, according to the three preceding conditions. These are the first conditions of the gospel. All who comply with them receive forgiveness of sins, and are made partakers of the Holy Ghost. Through these conditions, they become the adopted sons and daughters of God. Through this process they are born again, first of water, and then of the Spirit, and become children of the kingdom—heirs of God—saints of the Most High—the church of the first-born—the elect people, and heirs to a celestial inheritance, eternal in the presence of God.

"It is the duty and privilege of the saints thus organized upon the everlasting gospel, to believe in and enjoy all the gifts, powers, and blessings which flow from the Holy Spirit—such, for instance, as the gifts of revelation, prophecy, visions, the ministry of angels, healing the sick by the laying on of hands in the name of Jesus, the working of miracles, and, in short, all the gifts as mentioned in Scripture, or as enjoyed by the ancient saints. We believe that inspired apostles and prophets, together with all the officers as mentioned in the New Testament, are necessary to be in the Church in these days."

The Mormons profess to found their faith and doctrine, and their system of theocracy, upon the common Bible and Book of Mormon. Very profound reverence is paid by the disciples to the following portion of the latter authority, giving an account of Christ's descent from heaven among the ancient Nephites in the wilderness—(from first edition, Book of Mormon, p. 476):

"And now it came to pass that there were a great multitude gathered together, of the people of Nephi, round about the temple which was in the land Bountiful, and they were marvelling and wondering one with another, and were showing one to another the great and marvellous change which had taken place; and they were also conversing about this Jesus Christ, of which the sign had been given, concerning his death.

"And it came to pass that while they were thus conversing one with another, they heard a voice, as if it came out of heaven; and they cast their eyes round about, for they understood not the voice which they heard; and it was not a harsh voice, neither was it a loud voice; nevertheless, and notwithstanding it being a small voice, it did pierce them that did hear, to the centre, insomuch that there was no part of their frame that it did not cause to quake; yea, it did pierce them to the very soul, and did cause their hearts to burn. And it came to pass that again they heard the voice, and they understood it not; and again the third time they did hear the voice, and did open their ears to hear it; and their eyes were toward the sound thereof; and they did look steadfastly toward heaven, from whence the sound came; and behold, the third time they did understand the voice which they heard; and it saith unto them, Behold, my beloved Son, in whom I am well pleased, in whom I have glorified my name: hear ye him.

"And it came to pass as they understood, they cast their eyes up again toward heaven, and behold, they saw a man descending out of heaven; and he was clothed in a white robe, and he came down and stood in the midst of them, and the eyes of the whole multitude were turned upon him, and they durst not open their mouths, even one to another, and wist not what it meant; for they thought it was an angel that had appeared unto them.

"And it came to pass, that he stretched forth his hand, and spake unto the people, saying: Behold, I am Jesus Christ, of which the prophets testified, that should come into the world; and behold, I am the light and the life of the world, and I have drank out of that bitter cup which the Father hath given me, and have glorified the Father in taking upon me the sins of the world, in the which I have suffered the will of the Father in all things, from the beginning.

"And it came to pass that when Jesus had spake these words, the whole multitude fell to the earth, for they remembered that it had been prophesied among them that Christ should show himself unto them after his ascension into heaven.

"And it came to pass that the Lord spake unto them, saying: Arise and come forth unto me, that ye may thrust your hands into my side, and also that ye may feel the prints of the nails in my hands, and in my feet, that ye may know that I am the God of Israel, and the God of the whole earth, and have been slain for the sins of the world.

"And it came to pass that the multitude went forth, and thrust their hands into his side, and did feel the prints of the nails in his hands and in his feet; and this they did do, going forth one by one, until they had all gone forth, and did see with their eyes, and did feel with their hands, and did know of a surety, and did bear record, that it was he of whom it was written by the prophets that should come.

"And it came to pass that when they had all gone forth, and had witnessed for themselves, they did cry out with one accord, saying, Hosanna! Blessed be the name of the Most High God! And they did fall down at the feet of Jesus, and did worship him.

"And it came to pass that he spake unto Nephi, (for Nephi was among the multitude,) and he commanded him that he should come forth. And Nephi arose and went forth and bowed himself before the Lord, and he did kiss his feet. And the Lord commanded him that he should arise. And he arose and stood before him. And the Lord said unto him, I give unto you power that ye shall baptize this people, when I am again ascended into heaven.

"And again the Lord called others, and said unto them likewise; and he gave unto them power to baptize. And he saith unto them, On this wise shall ye baptize; and there shall be no disputations among you. Verily I say unto you, that whoso repenteth of his sins through your words, and desireth to be baptized in my name, on this wise shall ye baptize them: Behold, ye shall go down and stand in the water, and in my name shall ye baptize them. And now behold, these are the words which ye shall say, calling them by name, saying: Having authority given me of Jesus Christ, I baptize you in the name of the Father, and of the Son, and of the Holy Ghost. Amen. And then shall ye immerse them in the water, and come forth again out of the water. And after this manner shall ye baptize in my name, for behold, verily I say unto you, that the Father, and the Son, and the Holy

Ghost, are one; and I am in the Father, and the Father in me, and the Father and I are one. And according as I have commanded you, thus shall ye baptize. And there shall be no disputations among you, as there hath hitherto been; neither shall there be disputations among you concerning the points of my doctrine, as there hath hitherto been; for verily, verily, I say unto you, he that hath the spirit of contention is not of me, but is of the devil, which is the father of contention, and he stirreth up the hearts of men to contend with anger, one with another. . . . . I bear record of the Father, and the Father beareth record of me, and the Holy Ghost beareth record of the Father and me, and I bear record that the Father commandeth all men, everywhere, to repent and believe in me; and whoso believeth in me, and is baptized, the same shall be saved; and they are they which shall inherit the kingdom of God. And whoso believeth not in me, and is not baptized, shall be damned. . . . . Therefore, go forth unto this people, and declare the words which I have spoken unto the ends of the earth.

"And it came to pass that when Jesus had spoken these words unto Nephi, and to those which had been called, (now the number of them which had been called and received power and authority to baptize were twelve,) and behold he stretched forth his hand unto the multitude, and cried unto them, saying: Blessed are ye if ye shall give heed unto the words of these twelve which I have chosen from among you to minister unto you, and to be your servants; and unto them I have given power, that they may baptize you with water; and after that ye are baptized with water, behold I will baptize you with fire and with the Holy Ghost; therefore, blessed are ye if ye shall believe in me and be baptized, after that ye have seen me, and know that I am."

[Here follows in continuation nearly the whole of Christ's Sermon on the Mount, as plagiarized from Matthew, with some immaterial alterations, omitting the verse divisions and numbers.]

A Mormon temple was erected at Kirtland, at a cost of about fifty thousand dollars, by contributions in money and labor obtained from the saints through the resistless power of Smith's revelation process.

Mormonism, however, became distasteful to the unconverted people of Ohio, and especially obnoxious to the outside inhabitants residing at and near Kirtland. These outsiders were familiar, by information, with the source and history of the "Golden Bible" scheme, and scorned the impostor as beyond the public tolerance. The saints became involved in accusations of immoral and criminal practices—to which, with the feeling mentioned, and the general exceptionable demeanor of the leaders, may be traced the popular opprobrium rising against the sect. Moreover, the "promised land" had been looked for in a more western region, and probably Kirtland had never been fixed upon as a permanent locality for the saints. The two facts combined to determine the Mormon authorities upon a voluntary change of headquarters.

Rigdon and Cowdery had been sent forward as missionaries and explorers to find a place for the future Zion, and on their return reported in favor of Jackson County, Missouri. Smith and Rigdon repaired there to further view the situation, and they concurred in the selection, and fixed upon the spot now called Independence, in that county. The occasion called forth the following revelation in August of the same year:

"Hearken, O ye elders of my Church, saith the Lord your God, who have assembled yourselves together, according to my commandments, in this land which is the land of Missouri, which is the land which I have appointed and consecrated for the gathering of the saints. Wherefore, this is the land of promise, and the place for the city of Zion. Behold, the place which is now called Independence is the centre place, and the spot for the temple is lying westward, upon a lot which is not far from the court-house; wherefore it is wisdom that the land should be purchased by the saints; and also my tract lying westward, even unto the line running between Jew* and Gentile; and also

* Lamanite?

my tract bordering by the prairies, inasmuch as my disciples are enabled to buy lands. Behold, this is wisdom, that they may obtain it for an everlasting inheritance. He that sendeth up treasures unto the land of Zion shall receive an inheritance in this world, and his works shall follow him, and also reward in the world to come. Let all the moneys that can be spared, it mattereth not whether it be little or much, be sent up into the land of Zion, unto them whom I have appointed to receive."

A large tract of land was accordingly purchased at the locality selected; a town site was laid out, which they named Independence; a division of the Mormons removed there, and the work of upbuilding was commenced at once and vigorously prosecuted.

CHAPTER XI.

Mormons in Missouri—Their Prosperity and Adversity—Failure of Smith's Bank at Kirtland—The Prophet and Young flee to Missouri—Mob Conflicts—Interposition of Government Authorities—The Saints driven out of the State—Scattered Tribes—Asylum at Nauvoo.

IN 1834, most of the Mormons of Ohio had joined their brethren at Independence, Mo. They at once engaged in industrial pursuits, many of them proceeding to convert new lands into cultivated farms, while the mechanics, artisans, and others, pursued their appropriate callings in conducting improvements at the centre. The town sprang up in quick time, with the various establishments of industry necessary for employment and prosperity, including a printing-office, conducted by W. W. Phelps, late of Canandaigua, N. Y. He published a sort of religious paper called the *Evening and Morning Star*, which was to be the adopted organ of the saints. Smith returned to Kirtland, where Pratt and Young had remained, and where he proposed to continue his residence for several years, in order "to make money," as he said, for the benefit of the Church. He had there a sort of bank of issue, on what was then called the "wild-cat" principle, together with a store and a mill. He had, moreover, at Kirtland, a comfortable, well-furnished dwelling-house, which the "saints" had provided for him in obedience to revelation. He was, naturally enough, in no haste to part with these luxuries, and it was convenient for him to be "commanded of the Lord" to retain his dwelling-place as stated. Other Mormons, chiefly those with families, also remained behind, to work their farms and better prepare to join the new settlement.

Rigdon took the temporary lead at Independence, though he and Smith occasionally exchanged visits, and continued to act harmoniously together in the revelation business. At one period, however, during this separation by locality, an alienation between these worthies was apparently threatened by some cause not definitely understood; though this menace —perhaps unfortunate for both of them ultimately— was averted without an open rupture. Very likely the aspiring ambition of Brigham Young, who was with Smith at Kirtland at this time, was the chief agency in giving rise to some jealousies; but the threatened rupture, if permitted by Smith to occur, would have endangered if not blown up the whole Mormon project. And, of course, the culmination was averted.

Smith's banking and commercial enterprises at Kirtland finally resulted disastrously. His circulating medium had no redeeming basis, and was worthless in the hands of the people. His bank exploded, his mill stopped, and his store closed. These secular operations proved him an incompetent banker, an indifferent merchant, and a poor business-man. The popular excitement rose high against him and his religious pretensions. His effects in Ohio were hastily disposed of to the best practicable advantage, and in 1835 he accepted Missouri as his "promised land" and safer abiding-place. Young fled with him.

In the month of January, 1838, Smith and Rigdon, being at Kirtland together, were both arrested on charges of swindling, in connection with their worthless paper bank and other fraudulent operations. The suit was instituted by citizens who had become incensed by the perplexing losses they had sustained; and they were understood to be joined in the proceeding by some disaffected or "apostate" Mormons. The prisoners, however, escaped from the sheriff in the night, and made their way on horseback to Missouri. Smith gave the following version of the affair in the *Evening and Morning Star*, at Independence:

"A new year dawned upon the Church at Kirtland in all the bitterness of the spirit of apostate mobocracy, which continued to rage and grow hotter and hotter, until Elder Rigdon and myself were obliged to flee from its deadly influence, as did the apostles and prophets of old, and as Jesus said, 'When they persecute you in one city, flee ye to another;' and on the evening of the 12th of January, about ten o'clock, we left Kirtland on horseback, to escape mob violence, which was about to burst upon us, under the color of legal process to cover their hellish designs, and save themselves from the just judgment of the law. The weather was extremely cold, and we were obliged to secrete ourselves, sometimes, to elude the grasp of our pursuers, who continued their race more than two hundred miles from Kirtland, armed with pistols, etc., seeking our lives."

Before leaving Kirtland, the "saints" encountered schisms and dissensions among themselves, such as would have put an end to the progress of a less persevering people in a better cause. Renunciations, secessions, and apostasies, at this period in their career, had become common occurrences. And these troublous elements, as will be seen, were transmitted to Missouri, and indeed wherever they have had existence. Expulsions from the Church, and published proscriptions, have been the frequently occurring consequences, though restorations have been brought about when acceptable to the parties affected.

Martin Harris, it will be remembered, was the devoted follower and generous patron of Smith in the times of his greatest need. He supplied the material aid so necessary in starting the Mormon train. He paid for printing the original edition of the "Golden Bible," thus supplying the foundation of the Mormon Church; and he gave to Smith his wedding-suit, on the pretence of its being consecrated to the "missionary" service. He was, moreover, the sole "witness" approaching to credibility in the matter of the veritable existence of the metallic records. And notwithstanding the failure of the book-printing as an anticipated money speculation, he continued his liberal contributions to Smith, accepting as binding the latter's "revelations" from time to time requiring his coffers to be filled by the "saints." But Harris, becoming reduced in his worldly circumstances, fell into disrepute with his trusted friend, who complained of his extreme fanaticism, his loquacity and officiousness. He demanded higher "spiritual" consideration in the synagogue than was held to be consistent or safe by the prophet. The fanaticism that was so welcome when available in the raising of pecuniary means, was not at all the qualification required by the cunning Smith in the conductors of the imposture at its maturity. Appeals were made for recognition of the obligation imposed and the promises made at Manchester and Palmyra. But these appeals were unheeded by Smith. Having lost his property and his home in the incipiency of the "saint" speculation, the cheated fanatic was ungratefully discarded by the now comparatively affluent recipient of his early munificence.

The alienation was widened, and the feud became bitter. Smith posted Harris and others in the "Elder's Journal" in this form:

"There are negroes who wear white skins, as well as black ones—Grames Parish and others who acted as *lackeys*, such as *Martin Harris;* but they are so far beneath contempt, that a notice of them would be *too great a sacrifice* for *a gentleman to make.*"

Harris was expelled from the Church. He was, however, afterward awarded a restoration, which proffer of grace he declined, and permanently seceded from the Smith organization. He nevertheless maintained his adhesion to his Mormon faith. This is in accordance with his own declaration as made when he was last at the scene of his early delusion, in the summer of 1858. Then his condition was that of extreme poverty, being an object of deep-felt sympathy to the contemporaries of his days of prosperity. His last fixed residence is understood to have been at Kirtland.

Others of the pioneer "saints" found difficulties in their pathway. Oliver Cowdery, the amanuensis to the translator of the Golden Bible, and David Whitmer, another of the "witnesses" in this matter, appear to have been prominent among those falling into transgression and tribulation. At Independence, Rigdon publicly charged these men with being connected with "a gang of counterfeiters, thieves, liars, and blacklegs of the deepest dye," and with "deceiving, cheating, and defrauding the saints." And Hyrum Smith, who had been imprisoned in the Jackson County jail, wrote this certificate of character for Cowdery:

"Those with whom I had been acquainted from my youth, and who had ever pretended the greatest friendship toward me, came to my house while I was in prison, and ransacked and carried off many of my valuables; this they did under the cloak of friendship. Among those who treated me thus, I cannot help making mention of Lyman Cowdery, who, in connection with his brother, Oliver Cowdery, took from me a great many things; and to cap the climax of his iniquity, compelled my aged father, by threatening to bring a mob upon him, to deed over to him, or to his brother Oliver, about one hundred and sixty acres of land, to pay a note which I had given to Oliver for one hundred and sixty-five dollars."

Oliver Cowdery was afterward arraigned before the Church, and found guilty of the following among other charges:

"Seeking to destroy the character of Joseph Smith, Jr., by falsely insinuating that he was guilty of adultery.

"Disgracing the Church by being connected with the bogus business, as common report says."

Conviction and expulsion were the fate of Cowdery, in this instance; though he was shortly afterward received again into the bosom of the Mormon sanctuary, and continued his labors as an accredited "elder" of that persuasion.

In Missouri, after a brief career of prosperity, the history of the Mormons became one of almost continuous warfare with the citizens of the neighboring country as a community, and with the public authorities of their different localities and the State. Jealousies and dissensions among themselves aggravated their afflictions and their perils. But determination and perseverance, such as is repelled by no obstacles within human endurance, marked the character of Smith and his associate leaders to the last—Mormonism knowing no other motto than "onward," while its pursuit is possible.

The interests of their embryo town (Independence) having been confided to committees appointed for that purpose, who had been indefatigable in the prosecution of the required improvements, the place had come to contain about twelve hundred Mormons in 1834. At this early period of their Missouri history, the alleged licentious character and fraudulent practices of the "saints," added to some real or fancied offences in regard to the then existing slavery question, caused an excited state of feeling among the Missouri people against them. They were accused of stealing cattle and other property, of being connected with counterfeiting gangs, and of nearly all the various offences in the criminal catalogue.

A public meeting of the inhabitants of the surrounding towns was called to consider the subject of ridding themselves of the source of their annoyance. The meeting was held on the 20th of July, at which it was resolved to expel the Mormons from the State. What was characterized as an "indecent and libellous publication" had appeared in Phelps' paper, and this served to inflame still more the excited minds of the Missourians. Riotous scenes of violence followed. The printing-office was destroyed, several of the "saints" were tarred and feathered, and others were killed and wounded while defending their rights.

By the interposition of the local authorities, a temporary suspension of this mob violence followed, but the populace refused to revoke their resolution. The meeting reassembled on the 23d of July, in augmented and armed force, when the determination for the expulsion of the whole Mormon tribe from the State was unanimously voted. Conferences were held between the belligerents, resulting in an agreement on the part of the "saints" to remove from Jackson County as soon as practicable, reserving the privilege of an opportunity to dispose of their property and provide for removal. The agreement was in writing, and signed by the leaders of the two parties. The Mormons were to be allowed the time until the following spring to complete their part of the agreement.

In the interim, the governor of the State was appealed to by the Mormons for redress, and he advised them to apply to the courts. Accordingly, encouraged by this favor of the State, suits were commenced against several of the ringleaders of the mob; and having taken the advice of Smith at Kirtland, the aggrieved party resolved to disregard the forced treaty and maintain their ground. Further lawless violence was thus provoked; a sort of civil war took place; both parties were armed; and two Missourians were among the killed. The saints were overpowered.

The Mormons now hastily abandoned their position, most of them going into Clay County as a temporary refuge, expecting to return to Independence and resume their possessions there after judicial action should secure to them protection. The persecution endured by them enlisted in their behalf the general sympathies of the people, and brought in converts. They spread into Caldwell and Davies Counties, establishing the city of Far West in the latter county, and under the prevailing impulse continued for a while to prosper and multiply their numbers.

The Missourians "found in their midst an ignorant, clannish population, combined together by religious fanaticism, arrogant and overbearing in their pretensions, and completely under the control of a single will." The popular outside feeling again became excited against the tribe. This gave rise to a public meeting of the inhabitants in June, 1836, by which a resolution was passed admonishing the obnoxious community to leave the State—time being allowed them as before to harvest their crops and dispose of their property. The "saints," fearing the consequences of a different policy, agreed to the proposal.

In the mean time, the Mormons had not sold their property at Independence; and, under Smith's advice, refused to sell at any price, contending that "the Lord had said that Zion should not be removed out of her place; therefore the land should not be sold, but be held by the saints, until the Lord in his wisdom opens a way for their return." Criminal proceedings were instituted against those who had forcibly ejected the owners, and were in some instances lawlessly occupying the property.

Time passed; one provocation led to another; mob violence revived; the State militia was called out by the governor; both parties were armed; Smith determined to defend his legal rights at all hazards; and mortal combat was imminent. The sum and substance of the result was, the anti-Mormons achieved an easy victory. None were killed or seriously wounded on either side. The Prophet Joseph and his brother Hyrum, with some forty others of their party, were captured and imprisoned in the county jail. Thus ended this struggle, and the Mormons finally agreed with the State authorities that they would permanently leave the State. What heightened the difficulty of the Mormons in this, as in the former conflicts, was the fact of their having to encounter exasperated seceders among the most savage of their enemies.

General Clark, who commanded the Missouri State militia in this affair, said, in a dispatch to Governor Boggs, November 10, 1838:

"There is no crime, from treason down to petit larceny, but these people, or a majority of them, have been guilty of—all, too, under the counsel of Joseph Smith, Jr., the prophet. They have committed treason, murder, arson, burglary, robbery, larceny, and perjury. They have societies formed under the most binding covenants in form, and the most horrid oaths, to circumvent the laws and put them at defiance; and to plunder, and burn, and murder, and divide the spoils for the use of their Church."

In answer to this dispatch, the governor wrote to the general, that "the ringleaders of the rebellion should be made an example of; and, if it should become necessary to the public peace, the Mormons should be exterminated or expelled from the State."

The Mormons could not longer stem the tide of popular exasperation against them, and had no other alternative than to quit Missouri, which they did as speedily as possible. By agreement, commissioners were appointed by the Governor to sell their property, pay their debts, and aid them in removing. The Legislature appropriated two thousand dollars for this object, and liberal contributions to the same end were made by individuals. Many of the retreating families were in destitute circumstances, and could not have gone without great distress, but for the means thus supplied.

Thus reduced to fugitives and wanderers, the proscribed "saints" were compelled to scatter in different directions. Their condition would now challenge comparison with that of the "scattered tribes" of their Babylonish ancestors. They had almost come to doubt, indeed, that "the earth is the residence of the saints." Before the close of 1839 they had all been driven from Missouri.

Governor Boggs, in a special communication on this subject to the Missouri Legislature, in 1840, thus refers to the Mormons:

"These people had violated the laws of the land by open force and avowed resistance to them; they had undertaken, without the aid of the civil authority, to redress their real or fancied grievances; they had instituted among themselves a government of their own, independent and in opposition to the government of this State, that had, at an inclement season of the year, driven the inhabitants of an entire county from their homes, ravaged their crops, and destroyed their dwellings. Under these circumstances, it became the imperious duty of the executive to interfere, and exercise the powers with which he was invested to protect the lives and property of our citizens, to restore order and tranquillity to the county, and maintain the supremacy of the laws."

Leaving Missouri, the Mormons crossed the river into Illinois, most of them finding refuge in Hancock County—some of them, however, returning to Ohio, and a few of the repentant dupes withdrawing entirely from the brotherhood. The main body established themselves at the point on the Mississippi, in Hancock County, which they named Nauvoo.

Perhaps the occasion should not pass without the remark, that by enlightened people the Mormons were regarded as the victims of misguided vengeance in Missouri. The ruffianly violence they encountered at the hands of lawless mobs, in several instances eventuating in deliberate murder, finds no extenuation in any alleged provocation. The due process of law might have afforded adequate redress for the criminalities of which they should be found guilty on legal trial. Such was the view of the subject rightly taken by the people of Illinois and of the world, though it may have been wrongfully applied in favor of the cause of the persecuted.

CHAPTER XII.

Mormons settle at Nauvoo—Public Sympathy—Accessions and Conversions—City Charter—Revelations for Temple and Nauvoo House—Spiritual Wifeism and Polygamy.

IN 1840, Nauvoo had become the chief seat of Mormonism. The scattered "saints" had found a refuge on the Illinois side of the Mississippi, in Hancock County, which they named as above. They were generally welcomed and congratulated by the people of the surrounding country. Notwithstanding the atrocious character of the religious imposture pursued, and the false and delusive pretensions of its conductors, the cry of persecution, so well founded in truth, enlisted the public sympathy in behalf of the proscribed exiles from Missouri. The advantages of the situation were seized by Prophet Smith and his apostles and elders. Preachers and missionaries were put in active and efficient service, and vast numbers, both converts and unbelievers, flocked in to aid the enterprise of building up a new city. The perseverance and bravery that had been displayed by the leaders, and the endurance and enthusiasm evidenced by their ignorant and fanatical followers, amid all the varieties of their good and evil fortune, would have deserved high admiration in a meritorious cause.

From Brigham Young, Parley P. Pratt,* and others, who had been sent out from Ohio and Missouri as foreign missionaries, to spread the Mormon gospel to the uttermost parts of the earth, vividly encouraging accounts were received by Prophet Smith. In the spring of 1841, Young shipped from Liverpool to New York for the "promised land," seven hundred and sixty-nine of the faithful; and at the same time returned himself to Nauvoo, leaving in England, Scotland, and Wales, numerous churches with organizations completed, as the results of the labors of himself and his colleagues. The Book of Mormon had been republished and disseminated, tracts printed and distributed, religious papers established and circulated, and all the proselyting machinery set in operation in those countries, such as were calculated to convince and win the minds suitably constituted to receive the pretensions put forth.

These immigrants, followed by similar masses from abroad, were joyfully received at Nauvoo, rap-

* Pratt rejoined the Mormon brotherhood at Salt Lake, and was afterward assassinated by the exasperated husband of a woman who had been converted to Mormonism in Arkansas, in 1856. See Appendix for particulars.

idly augmenting the population of that "Saints' rest." Like accessions of foreign converts had been previously received in Missouri; and these, with others originally destined for that State, were turned to the new city. Mormonism was proving its claim as the grand focus of the fanatical element of the world.

Smith saw his opportunity and embraced it. He put forth a revelation, in which, among other requirements, a temple was commanded to be built, and the saints, far and near, were called upon to come forward with their gold, silver, precious stones, and property and means of every kind needed, and also with the labor of their hands to fulfil this "requirement of the Lord." The response was prompt and enthusiastic. In the same season, with imposing ceremonies, was laid the corner-stone of a temple, which was to compare in size and magnificence with Solomon's at Jerusalem. An effective lever in aid of this enterprise was the Mormon invention of the doctrine of "baptism for the dead," whereby the living could be baptized for the salvation of the souls of deceased friends. This, to be efficacious, must be done in a spiritually dedicated temple. The doctrine continues to be a prominent feature in the Mormon faith and practice.

A liberal city charter was obtained from the Illinois Legislature, in 1842, granting, among other extraordinary powers, that of raising a strong military organization. The "Nauvoo Legion," extending finally to an armed force of four thousand men, with Smith as the general in command, was one of the fruits of this State action. Smith superbly equipped himself, and called to his aid a splendid staff. At the last dress parade of the Legion, he was accompanied in the field by a display of ten of his spiritual wives or concubines, dressed in a fine uniform, and mounted on elegant white horses.

Mormonism was more than itself again, and things went on swimmingly. The "saints" were now estimated to number from twelve to fifteen thousand, in Nauvoo City and its vicinity. Smith had introduced the system of "spiritual wifeism," and had largely increased his household by celestial "ensealment." This was the preliminary step of polygamy, or its practical adoption, though it had not yet been revealed as a tenet in the Mormon creed. Howbeit, he wanted a house built for himself, and made a call upon his followers. It was a revelation for a hotel institution, in which he was to have his headquarters, concluding as follows:

"Therefore, let my servant Joseph, and his seed after him, have place in that house from generation to generation, for ever and ever, saith the Lord; and let the name of that house be called the Nauvoo House; and let it be a delightful habitation for man, and a resting place for the weary traveller."

This command, like all other communications from the same source, was accepted as of heavenly authenticity, and fulfilled with alacrity; for it was reasoned by his disciples, that "an uneducated man who could outdo all the wisdom of the world in translating the hieroglyphic records constituting the Book of Mormon, can be no other than an inspired prophet who is to be obeyed."

The Nauvoo House was built, and amply furnished, and Smith was at once its proprietor and chief guest. Suites of well-furnished rooms were appropriated to the use of himself and his family—most of his spiritual wives continuing to live at their respective homes, some of them remaining with their believing temporal husbands. He revelled in luxury, played the gentleman and the saint, hospitably entertained his friends, and became exceedingly popular in the Church and in the outside world. From the vagabondish, taciturn, penniless "Joe Smith," at the beginning of his Mormon scheme, he had become the rubicund, genial, affluent autocrat-prophet, of two hundred and twenty pounds avoirdupois, with forty wives all told. His children could not be enumerated with any degree of accuracy.

The great Mormon ruler, in addition to his extraordinary ecclesiastical prerogatives, was now (1843) commandant of the Nauvoo Legion, mayor of the city, and "monarch of all he surveyed." He aspired to yet higher dignity, and was announced in the *Times and Seasons* as a candidate for the presidency of the United States. He held correspondence with Clay and Calhoun upon grave national topics, especially in reference to the policy he ought to pursue if he should be elected. Thousands of his followers cherished an undoubting faith in the realization of such a result. By his tithing levies, he had amassed a fortune estimated at a million of dollars, as property was valued at Nauvoo. The number of converts, at home and abroad, was claimed to be one hundred thousand, and rapidly increasing.

Such is a glancing view of Smith's spiritual and temporal circumstances when the first revelation in favor of polygamy occurred. This heavenly communication, however, was for years withheld as a secret from all but the initiated dignitaries of the Church. It was not, indeed, generally admitted as a part of the religion of the "saints," until after the hegira to Salt Lake, when its first publication appeared by authority in the *Deseret News*, September 14, 1852. From that date it has been accepted as a fundamental tenet in the Mormon theology.

This subject may be regarded as a vastly important one, whether considered as the epoch of an institution under assumed religious sanctions, which is condemned by the laws and by the civilization of the age, or in reference to the ultimate consequences and perils to the sect immediately affected. Both on this account, and as a further specimen of the Smith-Rigdon adroitness in "revelation," the essential portions of the document are here inserted. As officially promulgated in the manner above stated, it is entitled—

"*Revelation given to Joseph Smith, Nauvoo, July 12th*, 1843.

"Verily, thus saith the Lord unto you, my servant Joseph, that inasmuch as you have inquired of my hand to know and understand wherein I, the Lord, justified my servants Abraham, Isaac, and Jacob; as also Moses, David, and Solomon, my servants, as touching the principle and doctrine of their having many wives and concubines: Behold! and lo, I am the Lord thy God, and will answer thee, as touching this matter: therefore, prepare thy heart to receive and obey the instructions which I am about to give unto you; for all those who have this law revealed unto them must obey the same; for behold! I reveal unto you a new and an everlasting covenant, and if ye abide not that covenant, then are ye damned; for no one can reject this covenant and be permitted to enter into my glory. . . . .

"And verily I say unto you, that the conditions of this law are these: All covenants, contracts, bonds, obligations, oaths, vows, performances, connections, associations, or expectations, that are not made, and entered into, and sealed, by the Holy Spirit of promise, of him who is anointed, both as well for time and for all eternity, and that, too, most holy, by revelation and commandment, through the medium of mine anointed, whom I have appointed on the earth to hold this power, (and I have appointed unto my servant Joseph to hold this power in the last days, and there is never but one on the earth at a time on whom this power and the keys of this priesthood are conferred,) are of no efficacy, virtue, or force, in and after the resurrection from the dead; for all contracts that are not made unto this end, have an end when men are dead. . . . .

"Therefore, if a man marry him a wife in the world, and he marry her not by me, nor by my word, and he covenant with her so long as he is in the world, and she with him, their covenant and marriage is not of force when they are dead, and when they are out of the world; therefore, they are not bound by any law when they are out of the world; therefore, when they are out of the world, they neither marry nor are given in marriage, but are appointed angels in heaven, which angels are ministering servants, to minister to those who are worthy of a far more, and an exceeding, and an eternal weight of glory. . . . .

"And again, verily I say unto you, If a man marry a wife, and make a covenant with her for time and for all eternity, if that covenant is not by me or by my word, which is my law, and is not sealed by the Holy Spirit of promise, through him whom I have anointed and appointed unto this power, then it is not valid, neither of force when they are out of the world, because they are not joined by me, saith the Lord, neither by my word; when they are out of the world, it cannot be received there, because the angels and the gods are appointed there, by whom they cannot pass; they cannot, therefore, inherit my glory, for my house is a house of order, saith the Lord God.

"And again, verily I say unto you, If a man marry a wife by my word, which is my law, and by the new and everlasting covenant, and it is sealed unto them by the Holy Spirit of promise, by him who is anointed, unto whom I have appointed this power and the keys of this priesthood, and it shall be said unto them, Ye shall come forth in the first resurrection; and if it be after the first resurrection, in the next resurrection; and shall inherit thrones, kingdoms, principalities, powers, and dominions, all heights and depths, then shall it be written in the Lamb's Book of Life that he shall commit no murder whereby to shed innocent blood. . . . .

"Verily, verily, I say unto you, If a man marry a wife according to my word, and they are sealed by the Holy Spirit of promise according to mine appointment, and he or she shall commit any sin or transgression of the new and everlasting covenant whatever, and all manner of blasphemies, and if they commit no murder, wherein they shed innocent blood, yet they shall come forth in the first resurrection, and enter into their exaltation; but they shall be destroyed in the flesh, and shall be delivered unto the buffetings of Satan, unto the day of redemption, saith the Lord God. . . . .

"I am the Lord thy God, and will give unto thee the law of my holy priesthood, as was ordained by me and my Father before the world was. Abraham received all things, whatsoever he received, by revelation and commandment, by my word, saith the Lord, and hath entered into his exaltation, and sitteth upon his throne.

"Abraham received promises concerning his seed, and of the fruit of his loins—from whose loins ye are, viz., my servant Joseph—which were to continue so long as they were in the world; and as touching Abraham and his seed out of the world, they should continue; both in the world and out of the world should they continue as innumerable as the stars; or, if ye were to count the sand upon the sea-shore, ye could not number them. This promise is yours also, because ye are of Abraham, and the promise was made unto Abraham, and by this law is the continuation of the works of my Father, wherein he glorifieth himself. Go ye, therefore, and do the works of Abraham; enter ye into my law, and ye shall be saved. But if ye enter not into my law, ye cannot receive the promises of my Father, which he made unto Abraham.

"God commanded Abraham, and Sarah gave Hagar to Abraham to wife. And why did she do it? Because this was the law, and from Hagar sprang many people. This, therefore, was fulfilling, among other things, the promises. Was Abraham, therefore, under condemnation? Verily, I say unto you, Nay; for the Lord commanded it. Abraham was commanded to offer his son Isaac; nevertheless, it was written, Thou shalt not kill. Abraham, however, did not refuse, and it was accounted unto him for righteousness.

"Abraham received concubines, and they bare him children, and it was accounted unto him for righteousness, because they were given unto him, and he abode in my law; as Isaac also, and Jacob, did none other things than that which they were commanded; and because they did none other things than that which they were commanded, they have entered into their exaltation, according to the promises, and sit upon thrones; and are not angels, but are gods. David also received many wives and concubines, as also Solomon, and Moses my servant, as also many others of my servants, from the beginning of creation until this time, and in nothing did they sin, save in those things which they received not of me.

"David's wives and concubines were given unto him of me by the hand of Nathan my servant, and others of the prophets who had the keys of this power; and in none of these things did he sin against me, save in the case of Uriah and his wife; and, therefore, he hath fallen from his exaltation, and received his portion; and he shall not inherit them out of the world, for I gave them unto another, saith the Lord.

"I am the Lord thy God, and I give unto thee, my servant Joseph, an appointment, and restore all things; ask what ye will, and it shall be given unto you, according to my word; and as ye have asked concerning adultery, verily, verily, I say unto you, If a man receiveth a wife in the new and everlasting covenant, and if she be with another man, and I have not appointed unto her by the holy anointing, she hath committed adultery, and shall be destroyed. If she be not in the new and everlasting covenant, and she be with another man, she has committed adultery; and if her husband be with another woman, and he was under a vow, he hath broken his vow, and hath committed adultery; and if she hath not committed adultery, but is innocent, and hath not broken her vow, and she knoweth it, and I reveal it unto you, my servant Joseph, then shall you have power, by the power of my holy priesthood, to take her, and give her unto him that hath not committed adultery, but hath been faithful; for he shall be made ruler over many; for I have conferred upon you the keys and power of the priesthood, wherein I restore all things, and make known unto you all things in due time.

"And verily, verily, I say unto you, That whatsoever you seal on earth shall be sealed in heaven; and whatsoever you bind on earth, in my name and by my word, saith the Lord, it shall be eternally bound in the heavens; and whatsoever sins you remit on earth, shall be remitted eternally in the heavens; and whatsoever sins you retain on earth, shall be retained in heaven. . . . .

"And again, verily, I say unto you, my servant Joseph, That whatsoever you give on earth, and to whomsoever you give any one on earth, by my word and according to my law, it shall be visited with blessings and not cursings, and with my power, saith the Lord, and shall be without condemnation on earth and in heaven, for I am the Lord thy God, and will be with thee even unto the end of the world, and through all eternity; for verily I seal upon you your exaltation, and prepare a throne for you in the kingdom of my Father, with Abraham your father. Behold! I have seen your sacrifices, in obedience to that which I have told you; go, therefore, and I make a way for your escape, as I accepted the offering of Abraham, of his son Isaac.

"Verily, I say unto you, A commandment I give unto mine handmaid, Emma Smith, your wife, whom I have given unto you, that she stay herself, and partake not of that which I commanded you to offer unto her; for I did it, saith the Lord, to prove you all, as I did Abraham, and that I might require an offering at your hand by covenant and sacrifice; and let mine handmaid, Emma Smith, receive all those that have been given unto my servant Joseph, and who are virtuous and pure before me; and those who are not pure, and have said they were pure, shall be destroyed, saith the Lord God; for I am the Lord thy God, and ye shall obey my voice; and I give unto my servant Joseph that he shall be made ruler over many things, for he hath been faithful over a few things, and from henceforth I will strengthen him.

"And I command mine handmaid, Emma Smith, to abide and cleave unto my servant Joseph, and to none else. But if she will not abide this commandment, she shall be destroyed, saith the Lord, for I am the Lord thy God, and will destroy her if she abide not in my law; but if she will not abide this commandment, then shall my servant Joseph do all things for her, as he hath said; and I will bless him, and multiply him, and give unto him an hundred-fold in this world, of fathers and mothers, brothers and sisters, houses and lands, wives and children, and crowns of eternal lives in the eternal worlds. And again, verily, I say, Let mine handmaid forgive my servant Joseph his trespasses, and then shall she be forgiven her trespasses, wherein she hath trespassed against me; and I, the Lord thy God, will bless her, and multiply her, and make her heart to rejoice.

"And again, I say, let not my servant Joseph put his property out of his hands, lest an enemy come and destroy him—for Satan seeketh to destroy—for I am the Lord thy God, and he is my servant; and behold! and lo, I am with him, as I was with Abraham thy father, even unto his exaltation and glory. . . . .

"And again, as pertaining to the law of the priesthood: if any man espouse a virgin, and desire to espouse another, and the first give her consent; and if he espouse the second, and they are virgins, and have vowed to no other man, then is he justified; he cannot commit adultery, for they are given unto him; for he cannot commit adultery with that belonging unto him, and to none else; and if he have ten virgins given unto him by this law he cannot commit adultery, for they belong to him, and they are given unto him; therefore is he justified. But if one or either of the ten virgins, after she is espoused, shall be with another man, she has committed adultery, and shall be destroyed; for they are given unto him to multiply and replenish the earth, according to my commandment, and to fulfil the promise which was given by my Father before the foundation of the world, and for their exaltation in the eternal worlds, that they may bear the souls of men; for herein is the work of my Father continued, that he may be glorified.

"And again, verily, verily, I say unto you, If any man have a wife who holds the keys of this power, and he teaches unto her the law of my priesthood as pertaining to these things, then shall she believe and administer unto him, or she shall be destroyed, saith the Lord your God; for I will destroy her; for I will magnify my name upon all those who receive and abide in my law. Therefore it shall be lawful in me if she receive not this law, for him to receive all things whatsoever I, the Lord his God, will give unto him, because she did not believe and administer unto him according to my word; and she then becomes the transgressor, and he is exempt from the law of Sarah, who administered unto Abraham according to the law, when I commanded Abraham to take Hagar to wife. And now, as pertaining to this law, verily, verily, I say unto you, I will reveal more unto you hereafter; therefore let this suffice for the present. Behold! I am Alpha and Omega. Amen."

CHAPTER XIII.

The Polygamous Revelation—Vices of the Saints—Criminations and Recriminations—Conflict with State Authorities—Assassination of Joseph and Hyrum Smith—Young succeeds to the Spiritual Dictatorship—Rigdon defeated and expelled.

THE interpolation of polygamy into what had been received by the disciples of Mormonism as their established religious and theocratic system, appears to have been put forth to the apostles and elders by Prophet Smith under great embarrassments. He knew it was a bold, if not a hazardous venture; for he was aware that his privy councils were divided upon the questions of expediency and safety involved. He feared that it might serve to open the blinded eyes of the honest zealots who were held spell-bound to his supposed inspired will. Moreover, he foresaw the scorn and detestation with which it was certain to be regarded by the Gentile world. A further reason, if not the more essential one, for apprehension and concealment, was probably found in the fact that by the law of Illinois the practice of polygamy was declared "bigamy," punishable by heavy fine and imprisonment in the penitentiary.

The occasion called for the exercise of extraordinary ingenuity, and his invention was this: To those of his believing councillors whose dissent he anticipated, he professed great concern of mind on account of the spiritual mandate under which he had been placed, and appointed a convocation of his council to take action upon the subject. When the time for assembling arrived, he went through the solemn farce of fleeing the city on horseback, rather than be the medium of communicating a revelation so repugnant to his mind! But he soon returned, with the awful story that he was met by an angel with a drawn sword, who commanded him, at the peril of instant death, to return and fulfil his mission. Of course he obeyed; such authority was not to be trifled with; and his estimate of the credulity of the superstitious minds he had to deal with was amply vindicated.

Another difficulty with Smith, perhaps, may have been found in the embarrassment which he felt in reconciling this polygamous revelation with the teachings of his own Book of Mormon:

"And were it not that I must speak unto you concerning a grosser crime, my heart would rejoice exceedingly because of you. But the word of God burdens me because of your grosser crimes. For behold, thus saith the Lord, This people begin to wax in iniquity; they understand not the Scriptures; for they seek to excuse themselves in committing whoredoms, because of the things which were written concerning David, and Solomon his son. Behold, David and Solomon truly had many wives and concubines, which thing was abominable before me, saith the Lord. Wherefore, thus saith the Lord, I have led this people forth out of the land of Jerusalem, by the power of mine arm, that I might raise up unto me a righteous branch from the fruit of the loins of Joseph; wherefore I, the Lord God, will not suffer that this people shall do like unto them of old. Wherefore, my brethren, hear me, and hearken to the word of the Lord; for there shall not any man among you have save it be one wife, and concubines he shall have none; for I, the Lord God, delight in the chastity of women; and whoredoms are an abomination before me."

Again, the same authority, in the plagiarism from Christ's Sermon on the Mount, has this passage:

"Behold, it is written by them of old time, That thou shalt not commit adultery; but I say unto you, That whosoever looketh on a woman, to lust after her, hath committed adultery already in his heart."

And still again, the Mormon book of "Doctrine and Covenants" contains the following ecclesiastical law in regard to marriage:

"You both mutually agree to be each other's companion, husband and wife, observing the legal rights belonging to this condition; that is, keeping yourselves wholly for each other, and from all others, during your lives."

The polygamists assume, however, to find authority for their apparent inconsistency, in the following passage of the Mormon scripture:

"For if I will, saith the Lord of Hosts, raise up seed unto me, I will command my people; otherwise, they shall hearken unto these things."

It must be by a very forced construction that the authority sought in the premises can be drawn from this text of the Mormon bible. The simple truth of the case is, that the revelation had become a "religious necessity." Smith, Young, Rigdon, Pratt, and others in the same dilemma, had proceeded too far in the mysteries of polygamy (practised under a different name), and the system had become too interwoven with their "latter-day" saintism, to admit of any alternative in their course, or continued concealment from the inner circle. Further explanation is deemed superfluous in this relation. A repetition of the offensive particulars already extant in the history of the parties implicated, and of the Mormon abomination generally, might seem more than is required by the public sense.

But at this era, saintly troubles were rapidly reviving and aggregating. Schisms, dissensions, and apostasies, were again rife in Mormondom. The Illinois people were intolerant and restive in view of the vices and criminalities in various forms ascribed to the latter-day hypocrites. These were necessarily the sources of acrimonious feeling and bitter hate between the conflicting communities. And to these causes, aggravated as they were by the partially transpiring polygamous revelation, with its concomitants and antecedents, may be traced the final event of the violent death of its author—which was followed in two years by the dispersion of the Mormon colony from Nauvoo. For, although as before explained, the practice of polygamy, then present and retrospective, with the existence of the Smith *dictum* itself, was positively denied by the guilty parties, and this, too, in a public sermon by Elder Pratt; the facts of the case were nevertheless sufficiently patent, both within and without the Church, to discredit the solemn averments of the Mormons in high places, and thus intensify the bitterness of the pervading feud.

From this time forward there was found "no peace for the wicked." Added to the common imputations of hypocrisy and imposture, charges of licentiousness, adultery, seduction, theft, dishonesty, and crime in greater variety than ever, were brought against the doomed leaders and their bigoted followers, both individually and collectively. Slander suits were commenced on the one side, and criminal proceedings instituted on the other. Litigation followed litigation, *pro* and *con.* Dr. R. D. Foster, a seceder (formerly of Palmyra, not one of the "pioneers"), charged Smith with the offence of spiritual "sealing" with his wife. Suits multiplied. Attempts to arrest Smith and other dignitaries of the Church were resisted by military power. The charge of treason was brought against the offending "saints." Still, Mormon defiance against the Illinois authorities was persisted in, and General Joseph Smith and his brother Hyrum, at the head of the Nauvoo Legion, opposed Governor Ford's State militia which had been called out to enforce obedience to law. The aspect was threatening. The governor, anxious to avoid the terrible slaughter impending, proposed to the Smiths a surrender as prisoners to the sheriff, and the disbandment of their legion as their only course of safety for their own lives and for their city. This proposal was finally acceded to, the governor promising them protection against violence from the excited populace on their way to jail and during their imprisonment. Accordingly, the legal arrest was made, and they were conveyed to the county jail at Carthage. Pursuant to the governor's treaty stipulation, the jail was placed under a military guard to protect the prisoners against the known existence of a prevalent avenging feeling, particularly existing on the part of Mormon dissentients whose domestic sanctums were alleged to have been invaded. Elder John Taylor and Dr. William

Richards were also arrested and placed in the same room with the Smiths.

The prisoners had been in the jail but a few days, when the governor's guard became reduced by the desertion of most of the men detailed, and late in the afternoon of the 27th of June, 1844, the remnant of the guard were overpowered by a mob of two hundred disguised and armed men, bent upon wreaking summary vengeance for real or imaginary wrongs. They broke open the prison doors, rushed in and fired upon the helpless inmates, killing the two Smiths, and wounding Elder Taylor severely. Dr. Richards escaped to tell the tale, which he did in the following language, dating June 27, 1844, as published in the Nauvoo *Times and Seasons:*

"A shower of musket-balls were thrown up the stairway against the door of the prison in the second story, followed by many rapid footsteps, while General Joseph Smith and Hyrum Smith, Mr. Taylor, and myself, who were in the front chamber, closed the door of our room against the entry at the head of the stairs, and placed ourselves against it, there being no lock on the door, and no ketch that was useable. The door is a common panel, and, as soon as we heard the feet at the stairs' head, a ball was sent through the door, which passed between us, and showed that our enemies were desperadoes, and we must change our position. General Smith, Mr. Taylor, and myself, sprang back to the front part of the room, and Hyrum Smith retreated two-thirds across the chamber, directly in front of and facing the door. A ball was sent through the door, which hit Hyrum on the side of his nose, when he fell backward, extended at length, without moving his feet. From the holes in his vest (the day was warm and no one had their coats on but myself), pantaloons, drawers, and shirt, it appears evident that a ball must have been thrown from without, through the window, which entered his back on the right side, and, passing through, lodged against his watch, which was in his right vest-pocket, completely pulverizing the crystal and face, tearing off the hands, and mashing the whole body of the watch; at the same instant the ball from the door entered his nose. As he struck the floor, he exclaimed emphatically, 'I'm a dead man!' Joseph looked toward him, and responded, 'Oh dear! brother Hyrum!' and opening the door two or three inches with his left hand, discharged one barrel of a six-shooter (pistol) at random in the entry; from whence a ball grazed Hyrum's breast, and, entering his throat, passed into his head, while other muskets were aimed at him, and some balls hit him. Joseph continued snapping his revolver round the casing of the door into the space as before—three barrels of which missed fire—while Mr. Taylor, with a walking-stick, stood by his side, and knocked down the bayonets and muskets which were constantly discharging through the doorway, while I stood by him, ready to lend any assistance, with another stick, but could not come within striking distance without going directly before the muzzles of the guns. When the revolver failed, we had no more firearms, and, expecting an immediate rush of the mob, and the doorway full of muskets—half way in the room, and no hope but instant death from within—Mr. Taylor rushed to the window, which is some fifteen or twenty feet from the ground. When his body was nearly on a balance, a ball from the door within entered his leg, and a ball from without struck his watch, a patent lever, in his vest-pocket, near the left breast, and smashed it in 'pi'; the force of which ball threw him back on the floor, and he rolled under the bed which stood by his side, where he lay motionless, the mob from the door continuing to fire upon him, cutting away a piece of flesh from his left hip as large as a man's hand, and were hindered only by my knocking down their muzzles with a stick; while they continued to reach their guns into the room, probably left-handed, and aimed their discharge so far around as almost to reach us in the corner of the room to where we retreated and dodged, and then I recommenced the attack with my stick again. Joseph attempted, as the last resort, to leap the same window from whence Mr. Taylor fell, when two balls pierced him from the door, and one entered his right breast from without, and he fell outward, exclaiming, 'O Lord, my God!' As his feet went out of the window, my head went in, the balls whistling all around. He fell on his left side, a dead man. At this instant the cry was raised, 'He's leaped the window!' and the mob on the stairs and in the entry ran out. I withdrew from the window, thinking it of no use to leap out on a hundred bayonets then around General Smith's body. . . . Mr. Taylor called out, 'Take me.' I pressed my way till I found all doors unbarred; returning instantly, I caught Mr. Taylor under my arm and rushed by the stairs into the dungeon or inner prison, stretched him on the floor, and covered him with a bed in such a manner as not likely to be perceived, expecting an immediate return of the mob. I said to Mr. Taylor, 'This is a hard case to lay you on the floor, but, if your wounds are not fatal, I want you to live to tell the story.' I expected to be shot the next moment, and stood before the door awaiting the onset."

The popular excitement ran high. The emotions were those of mingled indignation, sympathy, and vengeance. Nauvoo was in commotion. Precautionary measures were at once taken to prevent a general bloody outbreak. The Governor hastened to the scene, and, intensely wrought upon by the brutal murder that had been perpetrated in violation of the pledge he had given, sent orders to the Mormons to defend themselves if necessary, in the best manner possible, until he could send them protection. But further violence was happily averted.

The Governor published the following explanatory statement:

"I desire to make a brief but true statement of the recent disgraceful affair at Carthage, in regard to the Smiths, so far as circumstances have come to my knowledge. The Smiths, Joseph and Hyrum, have been assassinated in jail; by whom it is not known, but will be ascertained. I pledged myself for their safety; and upon the assurance of that pledge they surrendered as prisoners. The Mormons surrendered the public arms in their possession, and the Nauvoo Legion submitted to the command of Captain Singleton, of Brown County, deputed for that purpose by me. All these things were required to satisfy the old citizens of Hancock that the Mormons were peaceably disposed, and to allay jealousy and excitement in their minds. It appears, however, that the compliance of the Mormons with every requisition made upon them failed of that purpose. The pledge of security to the Smiths was not given upon my individual responsibility. Before I gave it, I obtained a pledge of honor, by a unanimous vote from the officers and men under my command, to sustain me in performing it. If the assassination of the Smiths was committed by any portion of these, they have added treachery to murder, and have done all they could to disgrace the State and sully the public honor.

"On the morning of the day the deed was committed, we had proposed to march the army under my command into Nauvoo. I had, however, discovered, on the evening before, that nothing but utter destruction of the city would satisfy a portion of the troops; and that, if we marched into the city, pretexts would not be wanting for commencing hostilities. The Mormons had done every thing required, or which ought to have been required of them. Offensive operations on our part would have been as unjust and disgraceful as they would have been impolitic, in the present critical season of the year, the harvest, and the crops. For these reasons, I decided, in a council of officers, to disband the army, except three companies, two of which were reserved as a guard for the jail. With the other company I marched into Nauvoo, to address the inhabitants there, and tell them what they might expect in case they designedly or imprudently provoked a war. I performed this duty, as I think, plainly and emphatically, and then set out to return to Carthage. When I had marched about three miles, a messenger informed me of the occurrences at Carthage. I hastened on to that place. The guard, it is said, did their duty, but were overpowered."

The bodies of the victims were taken to Nauvoo,

and their burial was attended with imposing solemnities. The immediate effect upon the Mormons of this appalling assassination was to cancel or wipe out of remembrance all the spreading vices of the lamented prophet, and throw a halo of glory around his character as a martyr who had sealed with his blood the truth of his divine pretensions. The outside public sentiment being terribly shocked by the catastrophe, sympathy in a large degree superseded the feeling of indignation and malice.

A writer in the *Christian Reflector*, at the time of the assassination, thus described the character of the prophet:

"Various are the opinions concerning this singular personage; but whatever may be thought in reference to his principles, objects, or moral character, all agree that he was a most remarkable man. Born in the very lowest walks of life, reared in poverty, educated in vice, having no claims to even common intelligence, coarse and vulgar in deportment, Smith succeeded in establishing a religious creed, the tenets of which have been taught throughout America; the prophet's virtues have been rehearsed in Europe; the ministers of Nauvoo have found a welcome in Asia; Africa has listened to the grave sayings of the seer of Palmyra; the standard of the Latter-Day Saints has been reared on the banks of the Nile; and even the Holy Land has been entered by the emissaries of this impostor.

He founded a city in one of the most beautiful situations in the world, in a beautiful curve of the 'Father of Waters,' of no mean pretensions, and in and about it he had collected a population of twenty-five thousand, from every part of the world. The acts of his life exhibit a character as incongruous as it is remarkable. If we can credit his own words, and the testimony of eye-witnesses, he was at the same time the vicegerent of God, and a tavern-keeper—a prophet, and a base libertine—a minister of peace, and a lieutenant-general—a ruler of tens of thousands, and a slave to all his own base passions—a preacher of righteousness, and a profane swearer—a worshipper of Bacchus, mayor of a city, and a miserable bar-room fiddler—a judge on the judicial bench, and an invader of the civil, social, and moral relations of men—and, notwithstanding these inconsistencies of character, there are not wanting thousands willing to stake their souls' eternal salvation on his veracity."

The Mormon *Times and Seasons* paid the following high tribute to the virtues of Smith—understood to have been written by his ever-faithful accomplice, Rigdon, who expected to be acknowledged as his spiritual successor:

"He was one of the best men that ever lived on earth. The work he has thus far performed toward establishing pure religion and preparing the way for the great gathering of Israel, in the short space of twenty years since the time when the angel of the Lord made known his mission, and gave him power to move the cause of Zion,* exceeds any thing of the kind on record. Without learning, without means, and without experience, he has met a learned world, a rich century, a hard-hearted, wicked, and adulterous generation, with truth that could not be resisted, facts that could not be disproved, revelations whose spirit had so much God in them that the servants of the Lord could not be gainsayed or resisted, but, like the rays of light from the sun, they have tinged every thing they lit upon with a lustre and livery which has animated, quickened, and adorned. The pages of his history, though his enemies never ceased to persecute him, and hunt for offences against him, are as unsullied as the virgin snow."

The temple, which, in an unfinished state, had been in use for some length of time, in conducting the religious services, spiritual-wife solemnities, and other mystic ceremonies of Mormonism, was completed in the fall of 1844, a few months after the death of the

* In this calculation of "twenty years," the writer dated back to the money-digging era, several years anterior to the Mormon invention. The palpable design was to persist in the after-thought invention that the "hidden records" had been revealed to Smith in 1823, before Rigdon's mysterious appearance at the scene, though they were not permitted to be taken until 1827. No such pretension was made until after Rigdon's connection with the imposture had become publicly known. It is only a piece of Mormon cunning.

Smiths. It was constructed of white limestone, one hundred and twenty-eight feet long, by eighty-eight feet wide, and two stories or sixty feet high, with a tower one hundred feet in height. Each of the two stories had two pulpits, to accommodate the Melchisedek and Aaronic priesthoods. There was a baptismal font in the basement, as authoritatively explained, "for the baptism of the living, for health, for remission of sin, and for the salvation of the dead, as was the case with Solomon's Temple, and all temples that God commands to be built." Its cost, raised by the tithing system, and computing the gratuitous labor bestowed under "revelation," was about a million of dollars.*

The soil of Mormonism had been fertilized by the blood of the Smiths. In any and every view of the subject, the murder was a great mistake as well as a great crime. A church founded in falsehood and hypocrisy has been strengthened, if not perpetuated, by its supporting influence. Indeed, it is rational to believe that, but for the opportunity thus afforded, to fasten in enslaved, superstitious minds, the impression of the "martyrdom" of their patron saint, the Mormon monstrosity would ere this have tottered to its everlasting fall and annihilation.

The general consternation having subsided, Mormondom became the arena of agitation and contest

* The temple was destroyed by fire in 1848.

for the dictatorship. Sidney Rigdon very naturally claimed the successorship by priority of inheritance, and assumed to fulfil its functions. Coequally with Smith, he had been associated with the origin and up-building of the Mormon Church and hierarchy. He was, equally with his deceased accomplice, the "author and proprietor" of the miraculously translated metallic book forming the basis of that power. He had ever been his predecessor's first counsellor and bosom friend, from the beginning of the grand experiment.

Brigham Young was alike ambitious; he disputed the pretensions of Rigdon, and aspired himself to the high position of "Prophet of the Lord." The strife became rancorous and unrelenting. Rigdon's reign was brief, and the termination of his career inglorious. Young was president of the Twelve Apostles, and was popular and influential in the Church. Rigdon lacked these elements of success, and was the inferior of his rival in the adroitness of demagoguism. Young denounced him as an impostor, and his revelations as "emanations from the devil." This spiritual and political warfare eventuated in Rigdon's expulsion from the Church, and he was formally "delivered over to the buffetings of Satan, in the name of the Lord. Amen." Young was unanimously elected to the presidency of the Church, and has ever since maintained his despotic sway.

Finally, Rigdon left the Mormons in virtuous disgust, and after halting awhile at his former residence in Pennsylvania, settled down in his present passive mood in Allegany County, N. Y., as has been stated.

William Smith, the only surviving brother of Joseph the prophet, also made an effort to assume the domination at Nauvoo; but, as in Rigdon's case, Young made short work with him, and his expulsion was the consequence.

Joseph Smith, third, the oldest of four legitimate sons of the late prophet, continues to live with his widowed mother, Emma Smith, near Nauvoo, in easy pecuniary circumstances. He claims to be the rightful head of the Church by inheritance, but is powerless against the indomitable will and all-pervading shrewdness of Brigham Young. He is opposed to polygamy, and denies the genuineness of the revelation on that subject attributed to his father.

It will thus be observed, that Mormonism has wholly passed from the direction of its original inventors and founders and their posterity, and become an independent and self-reliant institution.

The popular consideration in behalf of the "saints," which was the immediate corollary of the assassination problem, was brief in its duration. It was succeeded in the course of a year by a final determination, on the part of the Illinois people, to drive the whole tribe from the State; and they were compelled to seek a new home beyond the borders of civilization.

Young and his privy council accepted what appeared to be the popular conclusion, and made arrangements accordingly. They publicly announced their purpose, and the following is among their explanatory declarations to their followers:

"We, the members of the High Council of the Church, by the voice of all her authorities, have unitedly and unanimously agreed, and embrace this opportunity to inform you, that we intend to send out into the Western country from this place, sometime in the early part of the month of March, a company of pioneers, consisting mostly of young, hardy men, with some families. These are destined to be furnished with an ample outfit, taking with them a printing-press, farming utensils of all kinds, with mill-irons and bolting-cloths, seeds of all kinds, grain, etc.

"The object of this early move is to put in a spring crop, to build houses, and to prepare for the reception of families, who will start as soon as grass shall be sufficiently grown to sustain teams and stock. Our pioneers are instructed to proceed west until they find a good place to make a crop, in some good valley in the neighborhood of the Rocky Mountains, where they will infringe upon no one, and be not likely to be infringed upon. Here we will make a resting-place until we can determine upon a place for a permanent location.

"Much of our property will be left in the hands

of competent agents for sale at a low rate, for teams, for goods, and for cash. The funds arising from the sale of property will be applied to the removal of families from time to time, as fast as consistent; and it now remains to be proven whether those of our families and friends who are necessarily left behind for a season, to obtain an outfit through the sale of property, shall be mobbed, burned, and driven away by force.

"We agreed to leave the county for the sake of peace, upon the condition that no more vexatious prosecutions be instituted against us. In good faith we have labored to fulfil this engagement. Governor Ford has also done his duty to further our wishes in this respect. But there are some who are unwilling that we should have any existence anywhere."

The proscribed sect made the best and earliest practicable preparations for departure, and in February their first fleeing company, numbering sixteen hundred persons, crossed the Mississippi upon the ice with ox-teams, toward their western destination. The increasing exasperation of the Illinois people, and the consequent dangers of the situation, had led to a modification of the original plan of longer delay.

CHAPTER XIV.

Exodus from Illinois—Bold Adventure of Brigham Young—Sufferings on the Plains—Mexican War and Mormon Battalion—Arrival at Salt Lake—State of Deseret and Territory of Utah—Young declared "Prophet of the Lord"—Corner-stone of the new Temple.

BRIGHAM YOUNG directed the grand flight of the Mormons to an unexplored and unexpected region west of the Rocky Mountains. Their point of destination was in the deserts of California, then in Mexico, now in the United States Territory of Utah. Bands of young men as pioneers had preceded the general movement, for the purpose of exploring the route and providing the supplies and accommodations necessary for the wending caravans.

The emigrant trains, commencing their journey in February, 1846, and continuing their movements from Nauvoo until August of the same year, proceeded to a resting-place that had been selected for them upon the unoccupied prairies near Council Bluffs, where they mostly dwelt in tents during their sojourn.

Great suffering was experienced on the route, from fatigue, privation, and sickness; and here the sickness continued with even greater severity, being aggravated by the cholera, which raged with appalling mortality. And again complaints were heard of depredations upon the property of the scattering settlers. Roaming bands of Mormons were accused of stealing cattle from the grazing domains; and in this particular probably their Missouri history was prevented from repeating itself only by the sparseness of the population who complained of these aggressions.

The once flourishing Mormon city in Illinois, with its magnificent temple, luxurious Nauvoo House, spiritual-wife vagaries, polygamous harems, diversified Latter-Day-Saint institutions, and their superstitious devotees, was now left nearly a depopulated desert waste.

The news of the Mexican war met the emigrants at their resting-place near Council Bluffs. There was a call for volunteers. Young and his coadjutors had apprehended ultimate conflict with the Mexican authorities, and deemed it essential to be on good terms with the United States. Quick to perceive his opportunity, the great leader sent an agent to Washington with the tender of a volunteer battalion to the Government. It was accepted, and the men were speedily raised and sent to the field. Young received from the Government twenty thousand dollars for this patriotic demonstration, a large proportion of which sum was appropriated for his own private use and toward the material aid required in carrying forward his colonial enterprise. Accompanied by a party of devoted, hardy pioneers, with some of his elders, he then went westward upon an exploring expedition, to select a site for their future Zion, which they located in Great Salt Lake valley, where a preliminary survey was made for a city. A portion of their party returned to the temporary encampment in Iowa, to recommence the forward movement, the residue remaining to proceed with the preparatory improvements at the selected site.

The first companies of the emigrants, numbering about four thousand, arrived in the valley in July, 1847. The Indians received these people with hospitality. Indeed, no unfriendly demonstrations had been experienced from the savage tribes at any time during the journey. The Mormons had succeeded in favorably impressing them with respect to their friendly sentiments and spiritual endowments.

This grand adventure of Young and his followers, unprecedented for its boldness and success since the journeyings of their ancient "ancestors" from Jerusalem, is graphically described in Dixon's *New America:*

"Young advised his followers to yield their prize, to quit the world in which they had found no peace, and set up their tabernacles in one of those distant wilds in the far West which were then trodden by no feet of men, except those of a few red Indian tribes, Utes, Pawkes, and Shoshones, in what was called the American Desert, and was considered by everybody as no man's land. It was a bold device. Beyond the western prairies, beyond the Rocky Mountains, lay a howling wilderness of salt and stones, a property which no white man had yet been greedy enough to claim. Some pope, in the middle ages, had bestowed it on the crown of Spain, from which it had fallen, as a paper waste, to the Mexican republic; but neither Spaniard nor Mexican had ever gone up north into the land to possess it. In the centre of this howling wilderness lay a Dead Sea, not less terrible than Bahr Lout, the Sea of Lot. One-fourth of its water was known to be solid salt. The creeks which ran into it were said to be putrid; the wells around it were known to be bitter; and the shores for many miles were crusted white with saleratus. . . . .

"Trappers, who had looked down on the salt valley from peaks and passes in the Wasatch Mountains, pictured it as a region without life, without a green slope, even without streams and springs. The wells were said to be salt, as the fields were salt. Finding no wood and scarcely any fresh water in that region, these explorers had set their seal upon this great American Desert as a waste unfit for the dwelling and incapable of the sustenance of civilized men. But Young thought otherwise. He knew that where the 'saint' had struck his spade into the ground—at Kirtland in Ohio, at Independence in Missouri, at Nauvoo in Illinois—he had been always blessed with a plentiful crop; and the new Mormon seer had faith in the same strong sinews, in the same rough hands, in the same keen will, being able to draw harvests of grain from the desolate valley of Salt Lake. . . .

"Young knew that in crossing the great plains and in climbing the great ranges which are loosely clubbed together under the name of Rocky Mountains, the privations of his people would be sharp; but to his practical eye these sufferings of the flesh appeared to be such as brave men could be trained by example to bear and not die. Food and seed might be carried in their light wagons, and a little malt whiskey would correct the alkali in the bitter creeks. . . . .

"Pressed upon by their foes, they marched away from Nauvoo, even while the winter was yet hard upon them, crossing the Mississippi upon the ice, and started on a journey of fifteen hundred miles through a country without a road, without a bridge, without a village, without an inn, without wells, cattle, pastures, or cultivated land."

Young had not yet been accepted by the Church as "prophet, seer, and revelator," in the full celestial sense that had been recognized in the case of the martyr Smith. His appointment at Nauvoo extended only to the general successorship as first president in the ruling power of the hierarchy. He felt the embarrassment of his semi-prophetism. His "visions," as heavenly behests, were received with divided opinions; for he feared to attempt the enforcement of "revelations" or commands. Some murmurings had been heard relative to battalion-money questions, and these may have added to the delicacy of his position. He foresaw the dangers impending for the want of absolutism. As soon as reorganization was secured, he called a general meeting of the Church to consider the matter. Ascending the platform, he made solemn professions of "communion with the spirit of Prophet Joseph," at the same time going through with a series of impressive mimicries of his predecessor, in his peculiar style of theatric adroitness. The performance proved completely convincing to his audience. Ever since this successful experiment upon the superstitious elements of Mormondom, the pervading belief has been that the mantle of Joseph has fallen upon Brigham. By unanimous vote he was declared to be the "Prophet of the Lord;" and his despotic authority as ruler of the "Church of Latter-Day Saints of Jesus Christ in all the world," is undisputed by adhering Mormons. He appointed Heber C. Kimball and William Richards as his privy council, and these, with himself, constituted the trio called the "First Presidency."

Among the events of the Mexican War was the cession of California to the United States in 1848. Young, by superficial survey in 1849, established the State of Deseret, embracing a very large and scarcely defined domain; and Utah Territory was organized by act of Congress in 1850. The Mormon Deseret government was put in operation through the medium of a convention assembled under a proclamation of Young, about the time of the territorial action at Washington, and was constituted in the following manner: Brigham Young, Governor; Heber C. Kimball, Lieutenant-Governor; Daniel H. Wells, Chief Justice; together with a Legislative Council, which enacted a code of State laws. Young also received the United States appointment of territorial governor for Utah; and a Legislature for the Territory and a delegate to Congress were elected. The population of the Territory was composed almost wholly of Mormons and Indians, and the personal constitution of these preliminary governmental organizations could scarcely have been different.

In July, 1851, a full complement of Federal officers to fill unsupplied vacancies in Utah Territory, appointed at Washington, arrived and entered upon their respective official duties. Brigham Young and Heber C. Kimball were continued as Governor and Lieutenant-Governor, and their colleagues, were Lemuel C. Brandenburg, Chief Justice; Perry E. Brochus and Zerubbabel Snow, Associate Justices; Seth M. Blair Attorney-General; and B. D. Harris, Secretary.

Church and municipal affairs having become in a measure systematized, Governor Young issued the following "proclamation for a day of praise and thanksgiving," dated December 19, 1851:

"It having pleased the Father of all good to make known his mind and will to the children of men in these last days, and through the administration of his angels to restore the holy priesthood unto the sons of Adam, by which the gospel of his Son has been proclaimed, and the ordinances of life and salvation are administered; and through which medium the Holy Ghost has been communicated to believing, willing, and honest minds; causing faith, wisdom, and intelligence to spring up in the hearts of men, and influencing them to flow together from the four quarters of the earth to a land of peace and health, rich in mineral and vegetable resources, reserved of old in the councils of eternity for the purposes to which it is now appropriated; a land choice above all other lands; far removed from the strifes, contentions, divisions, moral and physical commotions, that are disturbing the peace of the nations and kingdoms of the earth—

"I, Brigham Young, governor of the Territory

aforesaid, in response to the time-honored custom of our fathers at Plymouth Rock, by the Governors of the several States and Territories, and with a heart filled with humiliation and gratitude to the Fountain of all good for his multiplied munificence to his children, have felt desirous to, and do proclaim Thursday, the first day of January, eighteen hundred and fifty-two, a day of Praise and Thanksgiving for the citizens of this our peaceful Territory, in honor of the God of Abraham, who has preserved his children amid all the vicissitudes they have been called to pass; for his tender mercies in preserving the nation undivided in which we live; for causing the Gospel of his kingdom to spread and take root upon the earth, beyond the power of men and demons to destroy; and that he has promised a day of universal joy and rejoicing to all the inhabitants who shall remain when the earth shall have been purified by fire, and rest in peace.

"And I recommend to all good citizens of Utah, that they abstain from every thing which is calculated to mar or grieve the Spirit of their heavenly Father on that day; that they rise early in the morning of the first day of the new year, and wash their bodies with pure water; that all men attend to their flocks and herds with carefulness, and see that no creature in their charge is hungry, thirsty, or cold; while the women are preparing the best of food for their households, and their children ready to receive it in cleanliness and cheerfulness; then let the head of each family, with his family, bow down upon his knees before the God of Israel, and acknowledge all his sins, and the sins of his household; call upon the Father, in the name of Jesus, for every blessing that he desires for himself, his kindred, the Israel of God, the universe of man; praying with full purpose of heart and united faith that the union of the United States may be preserved inviolate against all the devices of wicked men, until truth shall reign triumphant, and the glory of Jehovah shall fill the earth. Then, in the name of Jesus, ask the Father to bless your food; and when you have filled the plates of your household, partake with them with rejoicing and thanksgiving; and if you feel to make merry in your hearts, sing a song of thanksgiving; and lift up your hearts continually, in peace and acknowledgment of the unbounded mercies you are momentarily receiving. . . . .

"I further request, that when the day has been spent in doing good, in dealing your bread, your butter, your beef and your pork, your turkeys, your molasses, and the choicest of all the products of the valleys of the mountains, at your command, to the poor; that you end the day in the same order, and on the same principle that you commenced it; that you eat your supper with singleness of heart, as unto the Lord, after praise and thanksgiving, and songs of rejoicing; remembering that you cannot be filled with the Holy Spirit, and be preparing for celestial glory, while the meanest menial under your charge or control is in want of the smallest thing which God has given you power to supply; remembering that it is dependent on you for its comforts, as you are dependent on your God for your constant support.

"Retire to your beds early, that you may be refreshed, and rise early again, and so continue until times and seasons are changed; or finally, I say unto you, let the same process be continued from day to day, until you arrive unto one of the days of Kolob [where a day is one thousand of our years], the planet nearest to the habitation of the Eternal Father; and if you do not find peace and rest to your souls by that time, in the practice of these things, and no one else shall present himself to offer you better counsel, I will be there, and knowing more, will tell you what you ought to do next."

How far the expressions of loyalty to the Federal Union contained in the proclamation are to be received as having been sincere and honest at the time, is a question to be judged of in the light of the subsequent history of its author and of transpiring events.

Large accessions of emigrants sent forward by the foreign missionaries who had been selected from the ablest men of the sect, rapidly increased the Mormon numbers, in City and Territory. Many of these were farmers settling upon the free lands outside of the town. In 1854, the total number of converts in the valley and in all parts of the world, was estimated at half a million. At Salt Lake and in Deseret there was claimed to be forty thousand—probably an over-estimate, for the census showed only forty thousand two hundred and seventy-three total population in 1860.

Young had sent out an address to be distributed to the "saints" from all the Church and missionary stations, an extract from which will show the method and extent of the plan pursued:

"Come immediately, and prepare to go West, bringing with you all kinds of choice seeds of grain, vegetables, fruits, shrubbery, trees, and vines—every thing that will please the eye, gladden the heart, or cheer the soul of man, that grows upon the face of the whole earth; also the best stock of beast, bird, and fowl of every kind; also the best tools of every description, and machinery for spinning or weaving, and dressing cotton, wool, flax, and silk, or models and descriptions of the same, by which they can construct them, and the same in relation to all kinds of farming utensils and husbandry, such as corn-shellers, grain threshers and cleaners, smut-machines, mills, and every implement and article within their knowledge that shall tend to promote the comfort, health, happiness, or prosperity of any people.

"It is very desirable that all the saints should improve every opportunity of securing at least a copy of every valuable treatise on education—every book, map, chart, or diagram that may contain interesting, useful, and attractive matter, to gain the attention of children, and cause them to love to read; and also every historical, mathematical, philosophical, geographical, geological, astronomical, scientific, practical, and all other variety of useful and interesting writings, maps, etc., to present to the general Church recorder when they shall arrive at their destination, from which important and interesting matter may be gleaned to compile the most valuable works on every science and subject, for the benefit of the rising generation.

"Let all saints who love God more than their own dear selves—and none else are saints—gather, without delay, to the place appointed, bringing their gold, their silver, their copper, their zinc, their tin, and brass, and choice steel, and ivory, and precious stones, their curiosities of science, of art, of nature, and every thing in their possession or within their reach, to build in strength and stability, to beautify, to adorn, to embellish, to delight, and to cast a fragrance over the house of the Lord; with sweet instruments of music and melody, and songs, and fragrance, and sweet odors, and beautiful colors, whether it be in precious jewels, or minerals, or choice ores, or in wisdom and knowledge, or understanding, manifested in carved work, or curious workmanship of the box, the fir, and pine tree, or any thing that ever was, or is, or is to be, for the exaltation, glory, honor, and salvation of the living and the dead for time and eternity.

"The kingdom of God consists in correct principles, and it mattereth not what a man's religious faith is—whether he be a Presbyterian, or a Methodist, or a Baptist, or a Latter-Day Saint, or 'Mormon,' or a Campbellite, or a Catholic, or Episcopalian, or Mohammedan, or even Pagan, or any thing else. If he will bow the knee, and with his tongue confess that Jesus is the Christ, and will support good and wholesome laws for the regulation of society, we hail him as a brother, and will stand by him as he stands by us in these things; for every man's faith is a matter between his own soul and his God alone."

It is easy to comprehend the attractiveness of such an artful invitation to the thousands of ignorant and superstitious people addressed in the Old World, who seek the betterment of their temporal and spiritual condition in the "promised land" revealed to the Latter-Day Saints in America. These and kindred illusory appeals are turned to efficient account in the Mormon cause by the missionaries sent abroad in that work. In a tract published in England in 1851, by Orson Pratt, one of those emissaries designed to establish the "divine authenticity of the Book of Mormon," the author proclaimed the doctrine of modern miracles, and presented the claims of the new revelation in glowing terms. (Pratt has recently been expelled from the Mormon Church at Salt Lake by Prophet Young.) The following passage will suffice to show the winning character of this and other Mormon publications in foreign countries:

"The Latter-Day Saints know that Joseph Smith was a true prophet, and that the Book of Mormon is a divine revelation, because God has confirmed the same unto them by the miraculous manifestations of his power. There are now about six hundred branches of the Church of Christ in the British Islands, consisting of upward of thirty thousand believers, and between three and four thousand elders and priests. Now, there is scarcely a branch of the saints among this nation but have been blessed, more or less, with the miraculous signs and gifts of the Holy Spirit, by which they have been confirmed, and know, of a surety, that this is the Church of Christ. They know that the blind see, the lame walk, the deaf hear, the dumb speak, that lepers are cleansed, that bones are set, that the cholera is rebuked, and that the most virulent diseases give way, through faith in the name of Jesus Christ, and the power of his gospel. These are not some isolated cases that occasionally take place, or that are rather doubtful in their nature, or that have transpired a long time ago, or in some distant country; but they are taking place at the present period, every week furnishing scores of instances in all parts of this land; many of the sick out of the Church have, through the laying on of the hands of the servants of God, been healed."

Dixon gives the following description of the manner in which the immigrants are welcomed on their arrival at the Mormon capital, being a brief report of a "sermon" addressed to them by Young:

"Brothers and sisters in the Lord Jesus Christ, you have been chosen from the world by God, and sent through his grace into this valley of the mountains, to help in building up his kingdom. You are faint and weary from your march. Rest, then, for a day, for a second day, should you need it; then rise up and see how you will live. Don't bother yourselves about your religious duties; you have been chosen for this work, and God will take care of you in it. Be of good cheer. Look about this valley into which you have been called. Your first duty is to learn how to grow a cabbage, and along with this cabbage an onion, a tomato, a sweet potato; then how to feed a pig, to build a house, to plant a garden, to rear cattle, and to bake bread; in one word, your first duty is to live. The next duty—for those who, being Danes, French, and Swiss, cannot speak it now —is to learn English; the language of God, the language of the Book of Mormon, the language of these latter days. These things you must do first; the rest will be added to you in proper season. God bless you; and the peace of our Lord Jesus Christ be with you."

The Mormons have no negroes in their Church. They regard that race as the descendants of Cain, the first murderer, and the color of their skin as a curse put upon them by God. Hence all "Cainites" are excluded from their fellowship. Prophet Smith had in a single instance admitted one at Nauvoo, but the act was generally disapproved by the elders; though it was understood that the tithing exchequer was liberally benefited by the case, and perhaps for that reason its discussion soon ceased. The Cainite did not accompany the emigrants to Salt Lake, nor was his long continuance in Mormondom known to outside people. Furthermore, Young has been the declared advocate of negro slavery. In his first message to the Utah Legislature, his views upon this question were thus indicated:

"While servitude may and should exist, and that too upon those who are naturally designed to occupy the position of servant of servants, yet we should not fall into the other extreme and make them as beasts of the field, regarding not the humanity that is in the colored race; nor elevating them, as some seem disposed, to an equality with those whom nature and nature's God has indicated to be their masters, their superiors."

Probably the ancient Mormons of the times of Nephi had no knowledge of the "Cainites," for the records "hid up" by them, from the translations of which Joseph Smith, Jr., obtained the Book of Mormon, as pretended, furnish this text against slavery:

"But Ammon said unto him, It is against the law of our brethren, which was established by my father, that there should be any slaves among them."

Perhaps consistency, as between the professions and practices of the Mormon sect on this or any other question, should not be expected.

The Latter-Day Saints are modified millennarians. It is a theory interwoven with their belief, that the latter days are now passing. This is the burden of their preaching and revelations, and it is the mainspring of their proselyting machinery. All the original followers of Smith at Palmyra and Manchester, after the "Golden Bible" invention superseded the money-digging malversations, were avowedly influenced in their conversion to the "Mormon" gospel, more by this idea than any other receiving their serious consideration. And at the present time, in Utah and throughout the world, the faith of the "saints" is understood to be peculiarly strengthened by the revelation of Smith at Kirtland in 1833, to which they are pointed by the elders:

"And now I am prepared to say, by the authority of Jesus Christ, that not many years shall pass away before the United States shall present such a scene of bloodshed as has not a parallel in the history of our nation; pestilence, hail, famine, and earthquakes, will sweep the wicked of this generation from off the face of the land, to open and prepare the way for the return of the lost tribes of Israel from the north country. Therefore I declare unto you the warning which the Lord has commanded me to declare unto this generation, remembering that the eyes of my Maker are upon me, and that to him I am accountable for every word I say, wishing nothing worse to my fellow-men than their eternal salvation; therefore, 'fear God and give glory to him, *for the hour of his judgment is come.*' Repent ye, repent ye, and embrace the everlasting covenant, and flee to Zion before the overflowing scourge overtake you, for there are those now living upon the earth whose eyes shall not be closed in death until they see all these things which I have spoken fulfilled."

The believers, thinking they have seen fulfilled the first part of the prophecy of their martyr saint, are continually looking with undoubting faith for the verification of the remaining portion of it. Everywhere, Young's disciples believe that Mormonism is the true medium of salvation, and hence are rallying to the new Jerusalem in Utah as their only refuge.

The corner-stone of the temple at Salt Lake City was laid in February, 1853. There were about two thousand people in attendance, and the ceremonies were in the highest style of Mormon grandeur. Two brass bands participated in the exercises. Governor Young made the leading address on the occasion, the substance of which, as published, may be thus briefly stated: He said the "saints" were about to make their third attempt to build a temple to the Lord; that they had been twice frustrated in this duty by the powers of the devil, acting through the instrumentality of unrepentant gentiles, or at least that they had been only for a short season permitted to enjoy the one they had built at Nauvoo; that they were commanded to persevere, and that God had promised them his favor and protection when all their transgressions should be forgiven. He declared that the very ground where he stood had been revealed to him for seven years past as the spot where the temple should stand, and he intimated that its building might cost a million of dollars. He asked his followers to pay their tithes with cheerful promptitude, promising "God's blessing to them that do his will."

This oration was followed by a prayer by Elder Kimball, and by music from the band and vocalists. The Governor and the Twelve Apostles each threw up a few shovelfuls of earth, and a benediction ended the ceremony. The temple is planned for an immense building, calculated to seat eighteen thousand people. Its construction has not been hastened forward since the laying of the foundation walls. Young seems entirely content with the slow progress of the work, since it is the continual source of enriching revenues by the operation of the tithing system of the scheming beneficiary.

CHAPTER XV.

Political and Military—Recusancy of Young—He circumvents the Enemy—Clandestine Mormonism—Missionary Success—Statistics of the Saints—Utah, its Lakes and its City.

By the assumption of prerogatives not assented to by the Federal authorities of the Territory, Governor Young became involved in political controversies threatening the general peace. Among other abuses alleged, he was charged with misapplying the public moneys intrusted to his hands. The local legislative power, by the Mormon preponderance of the popular vote, was under his dictation and control. Twenty thousand dollars was appropriated by Congress and confided to him for expenditure in the erection of public buildings, more than one-half of which sum he was charged with putting directly into his own pocket, while he attempted to saddle upon the Government second-hand buildings worth less than the other half, but estimated by him at the price of the entire appropriation. Various other derelictions were alleged against the usurper; questions of jurisdiction arose; the difficulties multiplied from time to time; and the controversy between the Governor and his associate Territorial officers became warlike in its character. Colonel Steptoe arrived at the Mormon capital with a force of three hundred men, ready to enforce obedience to law. The contumacious Governor was prepared to meet this force with his Nauvoo Legion, should such culmination become necessary. Very soon he was removed from office by the President, and another appointment made to supersede him; but the new appointee declined the office, and Governor Young held over. In the mean time, he had plied his "saintly" arts of diplomacy with the belligerent commandant and his coöperating civil officers. The ultimatum was, that most of these Federal officers became friends of the Mormons—espoused their polygamous religion—and Young was reappointed Governor by their recommendation. Thus war in this instance was avoided—and Territorial affairs went on harmoniously.

Afterward, difficulties arose between the Mormons and anti-Mormons (the latter chiefly miners) in Western Utah, now organized as Nevada Territory, upon a question of jurisdiction. The signs were again ominous of war for a season; but finally Governor Young took counsel of his discretion, and peacefully withdrew from the contest. The questions involved in this matter were stated by Mr. Crane, delegate elect for Nevada, in January, 1859:

"The Mormons and anti-Mormons began the settlement of Western Utah in the latter part of 1854. The former, however, succeeded in 1855 in obtaining a numerical majority; and the Legislature of Utah, on being informed of this fact, organized the whole western part of the Territory, under the name of Carson County, and Governor Young appointed Orson Hyde, the President of the Quorum of Twelve Apostles, its Probate Judge. Soon after the judge arrived, adventurers from California, as well as from the Atlantic States, settled in Carson and other valleys on the eastern side of the Sierra Nevada, for the purpose of mining, farming, and raising stock. As they increased very fast, the Mormons became alarmed, and determined to expel them.

"They therefore ordered them to leave the country. Of course the anti-Mormons refused to do so. The Mormons then assembled their forces, and attempted to expel them, *vi et armis.* The anti-Mormons also organized, and fortified themselves, with a view of defending their lives and property against their assailants. For two weeks their armies camped nearly in sight of each other, without coming to a direct battle.

"By this time news had reached the miners in California of this state of affairs, and a large number had determined to cross the mountains, and afford protection to the anti-Mormons. On hearing this, the Mormons became satisfied that, unless they retraced their steps, they would themselves be driven from the country, instead of the anti-Mormons. They therefore proposed a truce, and agreed that all should enjoy a common heritage in that part of the Territory. . . . .

"The only remedy for this unnatural war, now raging between the Mormons and the anti-Mormons in Utah, is to be found in the immediate separation of these people under two distinct governmental organizations. One thing is inevitable—the Mormons and anti-Mormons will never, and can never live together in peace, under one government. The conflicts which took place between them in Ohio, Missouri, Illinois, and Iowa, and which are now going on in Utah, ought to convince any intelligent man of the justice and truth of this declaration. Indeed, the Mormons themselves acknowledge it; and so long as they adhere to their belief—a belief founded upon their own scriptures, that an absolute theocracy is the only government under which they can and should live—they never will be loyal to our government and countrymen; and hence their hostility to our institutions and people, and their inflexible devotion to their own.

"In every State where the Mormons have lived, it has cost the loyal people of the State thousands of dollars, as well as the loss of many lives, to compel them to obey the laws. In every instance they have resisted our laws, and in every State necessity demanded their expulsion.

"In Utah, while they were charged with the administration of the government and execution of the laws, they proved themselves not only traitors to our people, but treacherous to the Government, and openly rebelled against them and defied their authority, and it cost the Federal Government millions to conquer them. They have still control of the Territory, and they are inflexibly bent upon subduing the anti-Mormons of Western Utah; and if the latter are not separated from them, and protected by law, it will require the expenditure of millions more to restore order in Utah. Congress can count the cost in this matter, while we will have the melancholy duty of burying our dead. The people of Nevada will never be conquered—never be ruled by the Mormons. Come what will, they will resist to the bitter end. They prefer death to dishonor, and the Government may choose which of these shall be meted out to them.

"In addition to the above considerations, which should, I believe, present conclusive and imposing evidence, sufficiently satisfactory to induce Congress to organize the Territory of Nevada, I may likewise mention others. While the people of Western Utah have, in the Mormons, open and avowed enemies, they have likewise the savage tribes to defend themselves against. Some of these tribes are professed Mormons, while others are under their influence. Many conflicts have taken place between the anti-Mormons and some of these tribes, as well as between the emigrants (while crossing the Plains to the North Pacific) and the savages; and there is no hope of establishing amicable relations with these Indian tribes, until they are brought under other and better relations with the anti-Mormons of Utah. Peace does not reign in Utah, and never will, under the present order of things."

As above set forth, the Mormons were in hostile relations to the Government; they were, indeed, in actual rebellion. On that account, all the Federal authorities not in affiliation with them, had left the Territory. Yet a temperate policy was deemed advisable at Washington. Young was again removed, and a successor appointed, in the summer of 1857. The new appointments, altogether, were: Governor, A. Cumming; Chief Justice, D. R. Eckles; Associate Justices, John Cradlebaugh and Charles E. Sinclair; Secretary, John Harnett. These officers were supported by an army of three thousand men, under the command of Colonel A. S. Johnston. A sufficient history of affairs, as now presented, may be gathered from a report of the Secretary of War, December 5, 1857:

"The Territory of Utah is peopled almost exclusively by the religious sect known as Mormons. They have substituted for the laws of the land, a theocracy, having for its head an individual whom they profess to believe a prophet of God.

"This prophet demands obedience, and receives it implicitly from his people, in virtue of what he assures them to be authority derived from revelations received by him from heaven. Whenever he finds it convenient to exercise any special command, these opportune revelations of a higher law come to his aid. From his decrees there is no appeal; against his will there is no resistance. . . . .

"From the first hour they fixed themselves in that remote and almost inaccessible region of our territory, from which they are now sending defiance to the sovereign power, their whole plan has been to prepare for a successful secession from the authority of the United States, and a permanent establishment of their own. . . . .

"This Mormon brotherhood has scarcely preserved the semblance of obedience to the authority of the United States for some years past; not at all, indeed, except as it might confer some direct benefit upon themselves, or contribute to circulate public money in their community. It has, nevertheless, always been the policy and desire of the Federal Government to avoid collision with this Mormon community. . . . .

"Their settlements lie in the great pathway which leads from the Atlantic States to the new and flourishing communities growing up upon the Pacific seaboard. They stand a lion in the path, not only themselves defying the civil and military authorities of the government, but encouraging, if not exciting, the nomad savages who roam over the vast, unoccupied regions of the continent, to the pillage and massacre of peaceful and helpless emigrant families traversing the solitudes of the wilderness. The rapid settlement of our Pacific possessions; the rights, in those regions, of emigrants, unable to afford the heavy expenses of transit by water and the Isthmus; the facility and safety of military, political, and social intercommunication between our Eastern and Western population and States—all depend upon the prompt, absolute, and thorough removal of a hostile power besetting this path, midway of its route, at a point where succor and provisions should always be found, rather than obstruction, privation, and outrage. . . . .

"From all the circumstances surrounding this subject at the time, it was thought expedient, during the past summer, to send a body of troops to Utah, with the civil officers recently appointed to that Territory. . . . The instructions of the commanding officer were deliberately considered and carefully drawn, and he was charged not to allow any conflict to take place between the troops and the people of the

Territory, except only in case he should be called upon by the Governor for soldiers to act as a *posse comitatus* in enforcing obedience to the laws.

"An active, discreet officer, was sent in advance of the army to Utah, for the purpose of purchasing provisions for it, and of assuring the people of the Territory of the peaceful intentions of the Government. This officer found, upon entering the Territory, that these deluded people had already, in advance of his arrival, or of any information, except as to the march of the column, determined to resist their approach, and prevent, if possible, and by force, the entrance of the army into the Valley of Salt Lake. Supplies of every sort were refused him.

"The day after his departure from the city, on his way back, Young issued his proclamation, substantially declaring war against the United States, and at the same time putting the Territory under martial law."

Young, it will be seen, still assumed to be Governor of Utah, and in that capacity issued a proclamation of martial law. This document bears date September 15, 1857, and a few brief extracts will suffice to show its general spirit:

"Citizens of Utah: We are invaded by a hostile force, who are evidently assailing us to accomplish our overthrow and destruction. For the last twenty-five years we have trusted officials of the Government, from constables and justices, to judges, governors, and presidents, only to be scorned, held in derision, insulted, and betrayed. Our houses have been plundered and then burned, our fields laid waste, our principal men butchered, while under the pledged faith of the Government for their safety; and our families driven from their homes to find that shelter in the barren wilderness, and that protection among hostile savages, which were denied them in the boasted abodes of Christianity and civilization.

"Our opponents have availed themselves of prejudices existing against us, because of our religious faith, to send out a formidable host to accomplish our destruction. We have had no privilege or opportunity of defending ourselves from the false, foul, and unjust aspersions against us, before the nation. . . .

"We are condemned unheard, and forced to an issue with an armed, mercenary mob, which has been sent against us at the instigation of anonymous letter-writers, ashamed to father the base, slanderous falsehoods, which they have given to the public; of corrupt officials, who have brought false accusations against us, to screen themselves in their own infamy; and of hireling priests and howling editors, who prostitute the truth for filthy lucre's sake. . . . .

"Therefore, I, Brigham Young, Governor and Superintendent of Indian Affairs for the Territory of Utah, in the name of the people of the United States in the Territory of Utah, forbid—

"*First:* All armed forces, of whatever description, from coming into this Territory, under any pretence whatever.

"*Second:* That all the forces in said Territory hold themselves in readiness to march at a moment's notice, to repel any and all such invasion.

"*Third:* Martial law is hereby declared to exist in this Territory, from and after the publication of this proclamation; and no person shall be allowed to pass or repass, into, or through, or from this Territory, without a permit from the proper officer."

This proclamation met the United States forces on the Plains, dispatched from Fort Bridger by Daniel H. Wells, "commanding Nauvoo Legion," accompanied by his announcement of his purpose to carry out its instructions.

The able-bodied Mormons had promptly responded to their prophet's call to arms, and an army of ample numbers was found confronting the Federal troops. He addressed them in a Sunday-morning sermon, breathing the vengeance of war in earnest, as per the following specimen:

"This people are free; they are not in bondage to any government on God's footstool. We have transgressed no law, and we have no occasion to do so, neither do we intend to; but as for any enemies coming to destroy this people, God Almighty being my helper, they cannot come here. We have borne enough of their oppression and hellish abuse, and we will not bear any more of it, for there is no just law requiring further forbearance on our part. And I am not going to have troops here to protect the priests and hellish rabble in efforts to drive us from the land we possess; for the Lord does not want us to be driven, and has said, 'If you will assert your rights, and keep my commandments, you shall never again be brought into bondage by your enemies.' . . . .

"They say that their army is legal; and I say that such a statement is as false as hell, and that they are as rotten as an old pumpkin that has been frozen seven times, and then melted in a harvest sun. Come on with your thousands of illegally ordered troops, and I will promise you, in the name of Israel's God, that you shall melt away as the snow before a July sun. . . . .

"You might as well tell me that you can make hell into a powder-house, as to tell me that you could let an army in here, and have peace; and I intend to tell them, and show them this, if they do not stay away."

In the afternoon the Mormon autocrat gave further vent to his fury:

"Before we left Nauvoo, not less than two United States Senators came to receive a pledge from us that we would leave the United States; and then, while we were doing our best to leave their borders, the poor, low, degraded curses sent a requisition for five hundred men to go and fight their battles! That was President Polk; and he is now weltering in hell, with old Zachary Taylor, where the present administration will soon be, if they do not repent!

"Liars have reported that this people have committed treason, and upon their lies the President has ordered out troops to aid in officering this Territory; and if those officers are like many who have previously been sent here—and we have reason to believe that they are, or they would not come where they know they are not wanted—they are poor, miserable blacklegs, broken-down political hacks, robbers, and whoremongers; men that are not fit for civilized society; so they must dragoon them upon us for officers. I feel that I won't bear such cursed treatment, and that is enough to say—for we are just as free as the mountain air. . . .

"I have told you that if this people will live their religion, all will be well; and I have told you that if there is any man or woman who is not willing to destroy any thing or every thing of their property that would be of use to an enemy, if left, I wanted them to go out of the Territory. . . . .

"Now, the faint-hearted can go in peace; but should that time come, they must not interfere. Before I will suffer what I have in times gone by, there shall not be one building, nor one foot of lumber, nor a stick, nor a tree, nor a particle of grass or hay that will burn, left in reach of our enemies. I am sworn, if driven to extremity, to utterly lay waste, in the name of Israel's God."

The Federal troops were encamped at Green River, near Fort Bridger, one hundred and eighteen miles from Salt Lake City; and in November, Governor Cumming issued a proclamation to the people of Utah, informing them of his mission, which was to reorganize the Territorial government, bring the treasonable leaders to judicial trial, and enforce obedience to the United States Constitution and the organic law of the Territory.

The usual "ravages of war"—except those which result from fighting—were systematically perpetrated by the Mormon troops, such as stealing the Federal commissary stores, destroying the military wagons, and burning the forage and other means of sustenance for the "invaders." The winter was a severe one, and great suffering was experienced by the men on both sides, but no hostile gun was fired. Thus matters continued for a while, when, in December, Governor Cumming visited the city, on invitation of the Mormon leader, where he was received in a friendly manner by Governor Young. On mutual explanations, the latter relinquished the papers of his office, and gave a pledge of peace and obedience to law. A proclamation of Presidential pardon followed in June, accompanied by an assurance from the commissioners from Washington bearing the proclamation, in these words:

"If you obey the laws; keep the peace, and respect the just rights of others, you will be perfectly secure, and may live in your present faith, or change it for another at your pleasure. Every intelligent man among you knows very well that the Government has never, directly or indirectly, sought to molest you in your worship, to control you in your ecclesiastical affairs, or even to influence you in your religious opinions."

Peace now reigned; the new Territorial officers were at their posts; and the Federal troops marched unmolested through the city to their destined encampment at Cedar Valley, forty miles south.

Numerous instances of robberies, incendiarisms, and murders, have occurred from time to time upon the Plains, in which Mormons and Indians were implicated, sometimes in league. The details of these past atrocities do not necessarily come within the province of this volume.

Several vacancies in Territorial offices led to the following appointments, in February, 1863: Governor, Stephen H. Harding, of Indiana; Associate Justices, Thomas S. Drake, of Michigan, and Charles B. Waite, of Illinois. The opening for Governor Harding's appointment occurred in this wise: a Mr. Dawson had been appointed Governor, to fill a vacancy occasioned by the resignation of Governor Cumming, but becoming in some way entangled in the meshes of Mormonism after a brief official service, summarily resigned. As accused, he attempted the illustration of polygamy in a style not exactly in accordance with the mystic rites of the Church of Latter-Day Saints: whereat the prophet, the elders, and their followers, became intensely indignant. Apprehending personal danger, the clandestine polygamist sought safety in precipitate flight; but a self-appointed committee of the "Mormon boys" overtook him in a chase, gave him a severe castigation, and then set him free. That was Governor Dawson's last demonstration of Mormon faith, and the *finale* of his gubernatorial glory.

Congress passed an act "to punish and prevent the practice of polygamy in the Territories, and to annul certain acts of the Legislative Assembly of Utah." The Mormons held this act to be unconstitutional, as well as a violation of the pledge that had been given, and therefore refused to obey it as law. On the assembling of the Territorial Legislature, Governor Harding, in his message to that body, declared in favor of the enforcement of the act, discussing the question in a manner giving special umbrage to the polygamists. Extracts from the Governor's message:

"It would be disingenuous if I were not to advert to a question, which, although seemingly it has nothing to do in the premises, yet is one of vast importance to you as a people, and which cannot be ignored. I mean that institution which is not only commended but encouraged by you, and which, to say the least of it, is an anomaly throughout Christendom. I mean polygamy, or if you prefer the term, plurality of wives. In approaching this delicate subject, I desire to do so in no unkind or offensive spirit. . . . .

"I lay it down as a sound proposition, that no community can happily exist with an institution so important as that of marriage wanting in all those qualities that make it homogeneal with institutions and laws of neighboring civilized communities having the same object.

"Anomalies in the moral world cannot long exist in a state of mere abeyance; they must, from the very nature of things, become aggressive, or they will soon disappear, from the force of conflicting ideas.

"This proposition is supported by the history of our race, and is so plain that it may be set down as an axiom. If we grant this to be true, we may sum up the conclusion of the argument as follows: either the laws and opinions of the communities by which you are surrounded must become subordinate to your customs and opinions, or, on the other hand, yours must yield to theirs. The conflict is irrepressible. . . . .

"That plurality of wives is tolerated and believed to be right, may not appear so strange; but that a mother and her daughter are allowed to fulfil the duties of wives to the same husband, or that a man could be found in all Christendom who could be induced to take upon himself such a relationship, is perhaps no less a marvel in morals than in matters of taste.

"The bare fact that such practices are tolerated among you is sufficient evidence that the human passions, whether excited by religious fanaticism or otherwise, must be restrained and subjected to laws, to which all must yield obedience. No community can long exist, without absolute social anarchy, unless so important an institution as that of marriage is regulated by law. It is the basis of our civilization, and in it the whole question of the descent and distribution of real and personal estate is involved.

"Much to my astonishment, I have not been able to find any law upon the statutes of this Territory regulating marriage. I earnestly recommend to your early consideration the passage of some law that will meet the exigencies of the people. . . . .

"I am aware that there is a prevailing opinion here that the Act of Congress is unconstitutional, and therefore it is recommended by those in high authority that no regard whatever should be paid to the same; and still more to be regretted, if I am rightly informed, in some instances it has been recommended that it be openly disregarded and defied, merely to defy the same.

"I take this occasion to warn the people of this Territory against such dangerous and disloyal counsels. Whether the act is unconstitutional or not, is not necessary for me either to affirm or deny. . . . .

"The Constitution has amply provided how and where all such questions of doubt are to be submitted and settled, namely, in the courts constituted for that purpose.

"To forcibly resist the execution of that act, would be, to say the least, a high misdemeanor; and if a whole community should become involved in such resistance, would call down upon it the consequences of insurrection and rebellion." . . . .

The "pent-up fires of saintly wrath" now broke forth. The Legislature, largely Mormon in its composition, refused to print the message, and a large and excited meeting of the offended people appointed a committee to warn the Governor, and also the two justices counselling his action, to leave the Territory. At the meeting Young made one of his characteristic harangues, usually called "sermons." As authoritatively reported, he said, among other things in the same vein:

"You have just heard read the message of Governor Harding, delivered to the Legislative Assembly of this Territory. You will readily perceive that the bread is buttered, but there is poison underneath. When he came to Utah last July, the Governor sought to ingratiate himself into the esteem of our prominent citizens, with whom he had early intercourse, and professed great friendship and attachment for the people of the Territory. He was then full of their praises, and said he was ready to declare that he would stand in the defence of polygamy, or that he should have to deny the Bible; and stated that he had told the President, prior to leaving Washington, that if he were called upon to discuss the question, he would have to take the side of polygamy, or to renounce the authority of the Scriptures.

"In the face of all these professions, what has been the course of this man? . . . Man, did I say—thing, I mean—a nigger-worshipper—a black-hearted abolitionist is what he is, and what he represents; and that I do naturally despise. Do you acknowledge this man Harding for your Governor?"

Voices all through the audience responded, "No, *you* are our Governor."

"Yes, I am your Governor; and I will let him know that I am Governor; and if he attempts to interfere in my affairs, woe, woe unto him! . . .

"In regard to the war now desolating the country, it is but the fulfilment of the prophecies of Joseph Smith, which he told me thirty years ago."

The committee appointed to wait on the Governor and the two judges, and request them to resign their offices and leave the Territory, were John Taylor,

Jeter Clinton, and Orson Pratt. The following resolution was also adopted:

"*Resolved*, That we petition the President of the United States to remove Governor Harding, and Judges Waite and Drake, and to appoint good men in their stead."

In carrying out their instructions, the committee were met by expressions of defiance and contempt on the part of the officers addressed. The following is extracted from Governor Harding's reply to the committee:

"Gentlemen, I believe I understand this matter perfectly. I came here a messenger of peace and good-will to your people, but I must confess that my opinions have changed in many respects. But I came also, sirs, to discharge my duties honestly and faithfully to the Government, and I intend to do so to the last. It is in your power to do me personal violence —to shed my blood; but this consideration will not deter me from my purpose. If the President can be made to believe that I have been unfaithful to the trust he confided to me, he will doubtless remove me; and I then shall be glad to return to my home in the States, and will do so, carrying with me no unjust resentments toward you or any one else.

"But I will not be driven away; I will not cowardly abandon my post. I may be in danger in staying; but my purpose is fixed.

"Your allegations in this paper are false—without the shadow of truth. You call my message insulting, and you dare not print it, for fear your people may read it for themselves. To say that I have wronged you when I said that you are disloyal, is simply preposterous. Your own people—your public teachers and bishops—admit the fact.

"Let me say to you in conclusion—and as this is said to be a land of prophets, I too will prophesy—if, while in the discharge of my duties, one drop of my blood be shed by your ministers of vengeance, that it will be avenged, and not one stone or adobe in this city will be left upon another. I have now done, and you understand me."

The Governor's message was printed at Washington by order of Congress, and one thousand copies were distributed in Salt Lake City. No act of violence followed this political collision; and while Territorial government technically came to a stand-still, the Mormon theocracy with its obnoxious institutions went on without serious molestation. And indeed to this day, peace prevails in Utah, and the Congressional act prohibiting polygamy remains a dead letter.

Governor Harding, after about one year's service, was appointed Chief Justice of Colorado Territory, being succeeded as Governor of Utah by the appointment of James D. Doty, of Wisconsin, then Superintendent of Indian Affairs for the Territory. Judge

Waite resigned, and Judge Drake remained in office, on some terms of mutual conciliation.

The present statistics of Mormonism show the total conversions, at home and abroad, to be about one million, including those who have backslidden. Considered in connection with the singular origin of the imposture, as traced in these annals, the progress and results attained may be regarded as the wonder of the world. This Smith-Rigdon Church, based, as has been shown, upon Spaulding's fabulous history of "lost tribes," and beginning with the pioneer impostors in 1829, has now, in 1867, its believers nearly co-extensive with the bounds of civilization, and in some instances even beyond. The Mormons have their missions in England, Scotland, Wales, France, Italy, Germany, Denmark, Sweden, Norway, Switzerland, Malta, Gibraltar, Hindostan, Australia, Siam, Ceylon, China, Chili, Guinea, the West Indies, and the Sandwich Islands, with established churches in most of those countries. The Book of Mormon has gone through several English editions, and has also been published in French, German, Italian, Danish, Welsh, and Polynesian, with large editions of tracts in these different languages. Among the periodicals published by the Mormon Church, or in its advocacy, as the list was presented a few years ago, were *The Mormon*, at New York; the *Latter-Day Saints' Millennial Star*, published simultaneously at Liverpool and London;

the *Reflecteur*, in French, at Geneva; the *Étoile du Deseret*, in French, at Paris; the *Skandinavisk Stjern*, in Danish, at Copenhagen; the *Udgern Sion*, in Welsh; the *Western Standard*, at San Francisco; the *Zion's Watchman*, in Australia; and the *Deseret News*, *Telegraph*, and other publications, at Great Salt Lake City. Journals in English, Italian, Swedish, Spanish, and German, have since been established. Commissioners are exploring the Sandwich Islands with the view of acquiring by negotiation an ample tract of country for a future new Jerusalem, in case the necessity shall arise for vacating the present seat of the Mormon Zion in Utah.

The Mormon missionary system is prosecuted with great perseverance, and with corresponding success. Able and active men, mostly foreign converts, though numbers are sent out from Utah, are constantly employed in this service. At the present time there are no less than ten Mormon congregations in London, who hold their regular assemblages for public worship every Sunday. The London *Review* of a late date describes the Mormon emigrants sent from Europe to this country:

"The ignorant, untaught English and Welsh, generally too of dissenting religious opinions, if of any, form the staple of the recruits; and these are beguiled to a 'land flowing with milk and honey,' aided in their emigration, carefully watched as they set out, and tended when they arrive. From the day they leave London or Liverpool, till the hour they arrive, they are not left alone. Mr. Dickens saw one of their emigrant-ships, and while admiring its cleanliness, was struck with the utter reticence and silence of all upon the question of religion. The truth is, the 'saints' are told to hold themselves as saints, and to avoid talking with the gentiles. Their superiors or elders are always on the watch. They first entrap them, and then hoodwink them. During the voyage out they are well treated, and herein our own Emigration Commissioners might learn a lesson; but until the birds are caged, they really know nothing or very little of the trap they have fallen into. Hence many leave this country. Last year more than two thousand joined the false prophet. To supply this constant stream of emigrants, there is a large European mission, and in Europe, it is said, there are four hundred branches. In London and its environs we have 'meeting-rooms.' These places are generally shabby teetotal or dancing halls during the week, and on Sunday, an elder, with two or three companions to back him up, preaches in a low and vulgar style on religion, expounding the Proverbs or the Gospel even, and citing David or Solomon. Seldom or never is polygamy openly touched on; it is only to the matured Mormon, certainly not the stranger, that such a thing is broached. To conclude, such an agency is terrible in its results. We do not want a religious persecution, but we hold, with an astute American, that these people are contravening the law, not only of God but of the state, of knowledge, of health, of morals, and of nature."

And the London *Court Journal* tells a similar story, and regards this spread of Mormonism in many parts of England and Wales as "one of the saddest signs of the times." Among other facts it states (April, 1867), that "the son of Brigham Young is now in London on a proselyting expedition, and has been holding forth to large audiences in the tabernacle of the faithful. It is indeed startling to hear that many hundreds of women leave England every year for the Salt Lake City, and the statement is unfortunately true beyond all doubt."

The visions of the "promised land" in Utah, with the beauties of its "celestial city" in the valley of Great Salt Lake, have a winning influence as presented by the Mormon missionaries to the fanatical and discontented minds addressed in foreign lands. That interesting region, indeed, by the pioneer explorations and subsequent improvements of the Latter-Day Saints, has now a world-wide identity with our country's history, and is continually rising in importance to the Government and to Christendom.

It is believed that the Mormon emigration from the northern countries of the Old World will be larger this year (1867) than ever before. A well-informed writer remarks: "One of the chiefest means of conversion, of which the Mormon elders avail themselves, is the promise which they hold out of a home in Utah. The weary laborer and toil-worn mechanic of England can hardly resist the prospect of a country where their industry shall be properly rewarded, where land costs nothing, where their love of pleasure may be satisfied, and where every outward comfort and delight are sanctified by the encouragement of religious authority."

Mr. Bowles, editor of the *Springfield Republican*, in his graphic delineations entitled "Across the Continent," thus concludes a description of Utah and the Mormons as they are:

"This is Utah—these the Mormons. I do not marvel that they think they are a chosen people; that they have been blessed of God, not only in the selection of their home, which consists of the richest region, in all the elements of a State, between the Mississippi valley and the Pacific shore, but in the great success that has attended their labors, and developed here the most independent and self-sustaining industry that the Western half of our continent witnesses. Surely great worldly wisdom has presided over their settlement and organization; there have been tact and statesmanship in the leaders; there have been industry, frugality, and integrity in the people; or one could not witness such progress, such wealth, such varied triumphs of industry and ingenuity and endurance, as here present themselves. . . . .

"We came out upon the plateau, or 'bench,' as they call it here, that overlooks the valley of the Jordan, the valley alike of Utah Lake and the Great Salt Lake, and the valley of the intermediate Great Salt Lake City. It is a scene of rare natural beauty. To the right, upon the plateau, lay Camp Douglas, the home of the soldiers and a village within itself, holding guard over the town, and within easy cannon range of the tabernacle and tithing-house; right beneath, in an angle of the plain, which stretched south to Utah Lake and west to the Salt Lake—'and Jordan rolled between'—was the city, regularly and handsomely laid out, with many fine buildings, and filled with thick gardens of trees and flowers, that gave it a fairy-land aspect; beyond and across, the plain spread out five to ten miles in width, with scattered farm-houses and herds of cattle; below, it was lost in dim distance; above, it gave way, twenty miles off, to the line of light that marked the beginning of Salt Lake—the whole flat as a floor and sparkling with river and irrigating canals, and overlooked on both sides by hills that mounted to the snow line, and out from which flowed the fatness of water and soil that makes this once desert valley blossom under the hand of industry, with every variety of verdure, every product of almost every clime.

"No internal city of the continent lies in such a field of beauty, unites such rich and rare elements of Nature's formations, holds such guaranties of greatness, material and social, in the good time coming of our Pacific development. I met all along the plains and over the mountains the feeling that Salt Lake was to be the great central city of this West; I found the map, with Montana, Idaho, and Oregon on the north, Dakota and Colorado on the east, Nevada and California on the west, Arizona on the south, and a near connection with the sea by the Colorado River in the latter direction, suggested the same; I recognized it in the Sabbath-morning picture of its location and possessions; I am convinced of it as I see more and more of its opportunities, its developed industries, and its unimproved possessions. . . . .

"Salt Lake City is thus irrigated, mainly from one mountain stream; bright, sparkling brooks, course freely and constantly down its paved gutters, keeping the shade-trees alive and growing, supplying drink for animals and water for household purposes, and delightfully cooling the summer air; besides being drawn off in right proportions for the use of each garden. . . . Under this regular stimulus, with a strong soil made up of the wash of the mountains, the finest of crops are obtained; the vegetable bottomlands of your own Connecticut and of the Western prairies cannot vie with the products of the best gardens and farms of these Pacific valleys, under this system of irrigation. . . . I do not believe the same space of ground anywhere else in the country holds so much and so fine fruit and vegetables as the city of Salt Lake to-day.

"The soil of these valleys is especially favorable to the small grains. Fifty and sixty bushels is a very common crop of wheat, oats, and barley; and over ninety have been raised. President Young once raised ninety-three and a half bushels of wheat on a single acre. I should say the same soil located in the East, and taking its chances without irrigation, would not produce half what it does here with irrigation. Laborious and expensive as the process must be, the large crops and high prices obtained for them make it pay. Over all this country, that is forced to have an irrigated farming, there is no business that now pays so well, not even mining, and nowhere else in the whole nation is agriculture so profitable. . . . .

"There is a mountain of rock salt a few miles away; and below, in Arizona, is a similar mountain whose salt is as pure as finest glass. President Young showed us a brick of it to-day, that excited our surprise and delight as much as any novelty we have seen on our journey. . . . .

"The policy of the Mormon leaders has been to

confine their people to agriculture; to develop a self-sustaining, rural population, quiet, frugal, industrious, scattered in small villages, and so manageable by the Church organization. So far, this policy has been admirably successful; and it has created an industry and a production here, in the centre of the Western half of our continent, of immense importance and value to the future growth of the region. A few of the simpler manufactures have been introduced of late, but these are not in conflict with the general policy. There are three cotton-mills, confined to cotton yarns, however, almost exclusively, and one woollen-mill. Probably there are a hundred flouring-mills in the Territory also. Flour, the grains, butter, bacon, dried peaches, home-made socks and yarn, these are the chief articles produced in excess, and sold to emigrants and for the mining regions in the North. Probably two hundred thousand pounds of dried peaches were sold for Idaho and Montana last year. Hides are plenty; there is a good tannery here; and also a manufactory of boots and shoes. Cotton grows abundantly in the southern settlements; and experiments with flax, the mulberry tree, and the silk-worm, are all successful.

"As to mining, the influence of the Church has been against it. . . . President Young argues that the world has many times more gold and silver than it needs for financial purposes; that the country is poorer to-day for all the mining of gold and silver in the last twenty years; and that for every dollar gained by it, four dollars have been expended."

Salt and Utah Lakes are sketched by Mr. Ferris, late Territorial Secretary, in his "Utah and the Mormons:"

"Great Salt Lake is a very great curiosity. It is about one hundred and thirty miles long, and from seventy to eighty broad, and is, as near as may be, a vast collection of brine. The water seems to be saturated with salt to its utmost capacity of holding it in solution, indicating the neighborhood of great deposits of mineral salt. Between Great Salt Lake City and Bear River is a spring intensely salt, which pours out a volume of water equal to that at Spring Port, on the east side of Cayuga Lake, which it very much resembles. This is probably one of many others of a similar character which pour their contents into the lake. At particular points on the beach, where the regular course of the winds dashes up the waves, the salt collects in such quantities as to be conveniently shovelled into carts for domestic use. It is also procured by evaporation, three pails of the water producing one of salt. A person bathing may sit in the water, rising to his arm-pits, as in a chair; but let him beware of toppling over, unless he wishes to encounter the risk of drowning heels over head. The water is perfectly limpid, and has no living thing beneath its saline waves. It has many islands with high mountain-peaks, among the largest of which is Antelope Island, situated so near the eastern shore as to be accessible for grazing purposes, for which it is extensively used.

"Utah Lake, about forty miles south of Salt Lake, with which it is connected by its outlet, the River Jordan, is a handsome sheet of fresh water, some fifteen miles long by ten broad, and abounds with the finest salmon-trout. In approaching it from the north, the valley of the Jordan narrows, and in rounding a point about seven miles from the lake, a grand spectacle suddenly bursts upon the view of the traveller. The lake presents itself in placid beauty below him, surrounded, and seemingly completely walled in, by lofty mountains covered with snow. . . . .

"The Great Basin is rich in minerals, among which are iron and coal, found in Iron County, some two hundred and fifty miles south of Great Salt Lake City, in such abundance as to provide an adequate supply for the future wants of the population. . . . .

"Gold has only been discovered in Carson Valley, near the line separating Utah from California, but there are strong indications that it abounds in other portions of the Territory."

The great city of the Mormons in this modern "Plain of Jordan"—the Gomorrah of the nineteenth century—is depicted by Dixon, from personal inspection:

"The city, which covers, we are told, three thousand acres of land, between the mountains and the river, is laid out in blocks of ten acres each. Each block is divided into lots of one acre and a quarter; this quantity of land being considered enough for an ordinary cottage and garden.

"As yet, the temple is unfinished; the foundations are well laid, of massive granite; and the work is of a kind that bids fair to last; but the temple block is covered with temporary buildings and erections—the old tabernacle, the great bowery, the new tabernacle, and the temple foundations.

"The temple block gives form to the whole city. From each side of it starts a street, a hundred feet in width, going out on the level plain, and in straight lines into space. Streets of the same width, and parallel to these, run north and south, east and west; each planted with locust and ailanthus trees, cooled by two running streams of water from the hillside.

"Main Street runs along the temple front; a street of offices, of residences, and of trade. Originally, it was meant for a street of the highest rank, and bore the name of East Temple Street; upon it stood, besides the temple itself, the council-house, the tithing-office, the dwellings of Young, Kimball, Wells, the three chief officers of the Mormon Church. Banks, stores, offices, hotels—all the conveniences of modern life—are springing up in Main Street; trees have in many parts been cut down, for the sake of loading and unloading goods; the trim little gardens, full of peach-trees and apple-trees, bowering the adobe cottages in their midst, have given way to shop-fronts and to hucksters' stalls.

"Right and left from Main Street, crossing it, parallel to it, lie a multitude of streets, each like its fellow; a hard, dusty road, with tiny becks, and rows of locust, cotton-wood, and philarea, and the building-land laid down in blocks. In each block stands a cottage, in the midst of fruit-trees. Some of these houses are of goodly appearance as to size and style. Others are mere cots of four or five rooms, in which the polygamous families, should they ever quarrel, would find it difficult to form a ring and fight.

"In First South Street stand the theatre and the city hall, both fine structures, and for Western America remarkable in style. The city hall is used as headquarters of police, and as a court of justice. The Mormon police are swift and silent, with their eyes in every corner, their grip on every rogue. In the winter months there are usually seven or eight hundred miners in Salt Lake City.

"The city has two sulphur-springs, over which Brigham Young has built wooden shanties. One bath is free. The water is refreshing and relaxing, the heat ninety-two degrees.

"No beggar is seen in the streets; scarcely ever a

tipsy man; and the drunken fellow, when you see one, is always either a miner or a soldier—of course a gentile. No one seems poor. The people are quiet and civil, far more so than is usual in these Western parts.

"The air is wonderfully pure and bright. Rain seldom falls in the valley, though storms occur in the mountains almost daily; a cloud coming up in the western hills, rolling along the crests, and threatening the city with a deluge; but when breaking into wind and showers, it seems to run along the hill-tops into the Wasatch chain, and sail away eastward into the snowy range."

CHAPTER XVI.

Modified Theology—Young's Wealth—Polygamy and Spiritual Marriage—The Prophet's Harem—Mormon Abominations.

THE theology of the "saints" is subject to change by "revelation" at the caprice of the prophet. The latest version is given by Mrs. Waite:

"There are many gods, and they are of both sexes. But to us there is but one God—the Father of mankind, and the Creator of the earth.

"Men and women are literally the sons and daughters of God—our spirits having been literally begotten by God, in the heavenly world, and having been afterward sent to the earth, and invested with these tabernacles.

"God is in the form of man. He has a body, composed of spiritual matter. There is no difference between matter and spirit, except in quality. Spirit is matter refined.

"God is omnipotent, but not personally omnipresent. He is everywhere present by his Holy Spirit. His personality is generally expressed by the phrase 'He has body, parts, and passions.' He resides in the centre of the universe, near the planet Kolob. This planet revolves on its axis once in a thousand of our years, and one revolution of the Kolob is a day to the Almighty.

"Jesus Christ was the Son of God, literally begotten by the Father, and had the Spirit of God in the body of a man. After his resurrection, he had a body of flesh and bones only, typical of man's resurrected body. He differs in nothing from the Father, except in age and authority—the Father having the seniority, and consequently the right to preside.

"The Holy Spirit is a subtle fluid, like electricity. It is the subtlest form of matter, and pervades all space. By its agency, all miracles, so called, are performed. Miracles are simply the effects of the operation of natural laws. But they are laws of a higher character than those with which we are acquainted. This Holy Spirit is communicated by the laying-on of hands by one of the properly authorized priesthood, and the recipient is then enabled to perform wonderful things, according to his gift—some having the gift of prophecy, some of healing, some of speaking in unknown tongues, etc.

"There are three heavens—the telestial, the terrestrial, and the celestial.

"The telestial and terrestrial heavens are to be occupied by the various classes of persons who have neither obeyed nor rejected the gospel. The telestial is typified by the stars—the terrestrial by the moon.

"The celestial, or highest heaven, has for its type the sun, and is reserved for those who received the testimony of Jesus, and believed on his name, and were baptized by one having authority from him, and who afterward lived a holy life.

"The earth, as purified and refined, after the second coming of Christ, is to be the final habitation of those entitled to the glories of the celestial kingdom. Jerusalem is to be rebuilt, and Zion, or the New Jerusalem, is to be built in Jackson County, Missouri, whence the saints were expelled in 1833.

"There is a fourth class of persons, not entitled to either of these heavens. They are those who sin against the Holy Ghost; that is, those who apostatize after receiving the Holy Spirit. These go into everlasting punishment, to remain with the devil and his angels.

"The gospel, which people are called upon to obey, in order to gain a place in the celestial kingdom, is: first, they must believe in Jesus Christ as the Son of God, and in his authorized priesthood; secondly, they must repent of their sins; thirdly, they must be baptized by immersion for the remission of their sins; and, fourthly, they must receive the laying-on of hands for the gift of the Holy Ghost.

"God, having become nearly lost to man, revived

his work, by revealing himself to Joseph Smith, and conferring upon him the keys of the everlasting priesthood—thus making him the mediator of a New Dispensation, which is immediately to precede the second coming of Christ. All those who recognize the divine authority of Smith, and are baptized by one having authority, are the chosen people of God, who are to introduce the millennium, and to reign with Christ on earth a thousand years."

The Church organization, under the prevailing spiritual and temporal rule, is thus epitomized:

"*First.* The First Presidency. This consists of three, chosen from those who hold the high-priesthood and apostleship, and its office is to preside over and direct the affairs of the whole Church. It consists of a President and two Counsellors. .The President is also seer, revelator, translator, and prophet. He rules in all spiritual and temporal affairs.

"*Secondly.* The Apostles. These are to build up, organize, and preside over churches, administer the ordinances, etc.

"*Thirdly.* The Seventies. The quorums of the Seventies are to travel in all the world, preach the gospel, and administer its ordinances and blessings. There is, also, the Patriarch, whose duty is to bless the fatherless, to prophesy what shall befall them, etc.

"*Fourthly.* High-Priests and Elders. The high-priest is to administer the ordinances, and preside over the stakes of the Church; that is, over the churches established abroad. The elders are to preach and baptize; to ordain other elders, also priests, teachers, and deacons. All the foregoing officers are of the Melchizedek priesthood.

"*Fifthly.* The Aaronic priesthood, which includes the offices of bishop, priest, preacher, and deacon.

"The bishop presides over all the lesser offices of the Aaronic priesthood, ministers in outward ordinances, conducts the temporal business of the Church, and sits in judgment on transgressors.

"The priest is to preach, baptize, administer the sacrament of the Lord's Supper, and visit and exhort the saints.

"The teacher is to watch over and strengthen the Church.

"The deacon is to assist the teacher.

"There is also a High Council, consisting of twelve high-priests, with a president. The office of the council is to settle all important difficulties.

"The priesthood comes direct from heaven, and was lost to man, until the keys of both orders of the priesthood were given to Joseph Smith, by an angel from heaven, in 1829. After the death of Smith, they came into the hands of Brigham Young."

All these officers are but mediums for the transmission of the will of the president. Nor is it confined to spiritual affairs. Under the form of a church organization, this system absorbs not only the religious, but all the civil and political liberty of the individual member. The High Council forms an apparent check on the power of the president; but when it is considered that this body is composed of persons nearest the president, and under his immediate influence and control in other relations in the same organization—as high-priests, etc.—it will be seen that the check is only nominal, and forms no real protection to the rights of the people.*

The orders of the priesthood—the Melchizedek and Aaronic—are the same as adopted under Smith's administration at Kirtland, as before explained (chapter x.)

Brigham Young has reached his sixty-sixth year. As the ruling President of the "Church of Latter-Day Saints of Jesus Christ"—the successor of Joseph Smith, Jr., to the celestial pretensions of prophet, seer, and revelator—to the mandates of whose revelations all Mormondom yields willing obedience—his notoriety and power are scarcely second to those of his greater prototype, Mohammed. His wealth is understood to be immense, and is fast accumulating from tithes and speculations. His temporal riches consist of the precious metals, city and rural estates, government securities, and foreign investments. From the European mission alone he is said to have secured for

* "Mormon Prophet."

himself over half a million dollars in gold through the instrumentality of his tithing process. Many of the foreign immigrants bring large sums of money, all subject to his levies. The poor people suffer severely by the exaction; but in the steadfastness of their faith, they bear the oppression without an expressed murmur as a general fact.

The manifold wives and children of the prophet constitute his visible spiritual affluence. These blessings, like the first mentioned, cannot be computed with any proximity to accuracy, by the profane, perhaps not even by himself. From the best data attainable, his actual wives in polygamy—the women who live in his houses and in his harem—who are the recognized mothers of his children—are twelve in number, including his first or lawful wife. All but one of these have borne children to him, varying numerically from three to nine each, and aggregating in number to about sixty now living—all of whom are well provided for in respect to educational accomplishments and in other ways. Two of his elder sons have been employed in the foreign missionary service, and one of these, as elsewhere stated, was gaining converts in London, at the latest accounts. The spiritual or "sealed" wives of Young, it is said (probably with truth), cannot be counted by any authority; and at Salt Lake it is a very wise child that knows its own father,

Polygamy is not universal in Mormondom. The question of matrimonial plurality is governed by a man's pecuniary ability to support more than one wife, or by the choice of parties. But every member of the priesthood is expected to obey revelation in this particular, and all of the higher order have two or more wives each, the number being according to the grade of office or wealth of the elder. Heber C. Kimball and Daniel Wells, who, with Young, are the three constituting the "First Presidency," are next to the prophet in the scale of numerical wifery, though it is said there is no record kept in this department of their domestic relations. The Twelve Apostles have fewer blessings than their superiors, being thus stated on Mormon authority: Orson Hyde, four wives; Orson Pratt, four wives; John Taylor, seven wives; Milford Woodruff, three wives; George A. Smith (cousin of the late prophet), five wives; Amasa Lyman, five wives; Ezra Benson, four wives; Charles Rich, seven wives; Lorenzo Snow, three wives; Erastus Snow, three wives; Franklin Richards, four wives; George Q. Cannon, three wives. These statements do not embrace the spiritual ensealments of the apostles, but only the wives living in family unity. The numbers of their children are unknown.

This ancient Jewish institution of polygamy (practised only by portions of the Turks, Asiatics, Africans, North American savages, and Mormons), is the prolific source of schism and discontent among the "saints." Many of the backslidings and apostasies from the Church, estimated at an aggregate of twenty thousand, are traceable chiefly to this cause. Moreover, various combinations of dissenters have arisen for the same and other reasons, under the names of Strangites, Morrisites, Gladdenites, and Josephites, who occupy localities outside of the Salt Lake jurisdiction, under their own independent theocratic governments, while they neverthess adhere to the primitive Mormon faith. These have their separate leaders, denying as they do the pretensions of the prophet usurper.

Young is exceedingly revengeful against all apostates and those who in any manner question his divinity; and this last offence, unretracted, is certain to be punished by abandonment to the "buffetings of Satan." In a sermon on this head, the prophet expressed himself in this manner:

"When a man comes right out like an independent devil, and says, 'Damn Mormonism and all the Mormons,' and is off with himself, I say he is a gentleman by the side of a nasty, sneaking apostate, who is opposed to nothing but Christianity. I say to the former, 'Go in peace, sir, and prosper if you can.' But we have a set of spirits here worse than such a character" (alluding to doubters).

The revelation of Smith at Nauvoo in 1844, as

given elsewhere (chap. xii.), but first published at Salt Lake in 1852, forms the groundwork of the institution of polygamy as sustained by the Church under Young's administration. Prior to its appearance in the *Deseret News*, it was announced to the Church by Apostle Orson Pratt, and thus referred to by Prophet Young:

"You heard Brother Pratt state, this morning, that a revelation would be read this afternoon which was given previous to Joseph's death. It contains a doctrine which a small portion of the world is opposed to; but I can deliver a revelation upon it. Though that doctrine has not been preached by the elders, this people have believed in it for years."

Young's harem is a long, three-story frame building, including a stone basement. It has a spacious hall extending the entire length through the centre of each story, with rooms on either side for the occupants in their various employments. Its cost was about thirty thousand dollars, in addition to the free labor bestowed by command of the owner, "in the name of the Lord, and by the authority of the holy priesthood." Beside the private parlors and bedrooms for the wives and "other women," with the children, comprising the polygamous household, it has a spacious dining-room, a school-room, two receiving-parlors, a kitchen, weaving-room, laundry, coachman's room, etc. It has also a private office for the prophet, connected with which is his "*sanctum sanctorum*," or celestial bedroom, which is to be entered by no one without his special permission. Mrs. Waite, in her history of the prophet, gave the names and personal descriptions of twenty-four women who lived in the harem at the time of her recent residence in Salt Lake City, not including the first and lawful wife, with her children, who occupy a house by themselves. Most of the inmates have some sort of industrial pursuit—for "industry" is Young's motto—the various employments being cooking, washing, needlework, French and music teaching, poetry-writing, taking care of the children, receiving company, and attending to the diversified commands of the host of the harem.

There is also an endowment-house connected with the tabernacle, in which washings, anointings, spiritual-wife sealings, and other mystic ceremonies, are performed by those in authority.

The marriage law is thus explained: A man who has a wife already, must first seek the prophet's advice before making proposals for another, and through him obtain a revelation in favor of his intention; next he must obtain the consent of the parents, and then consult the lady herself. The president, in his discretion, may overrule any objection raised by the first wife, and either divorce her or "damn" her for persistence in her opposition. All things being ready for the solemnity, the parties—*i. e.*, the bridegroom and bride, with the legal wife—are arranged before the president of the Church:

"The president then puts this question to the wife: 'Are you willing to give this woman to your husband, to be his lawful and wedded wife, for time and all eternity? If you are, you will manifest it by placing her right hand within the right hand of your husband.' The right hands of the bridegroom and the bride being thus joined, the wife takes her husband by the left arm, as if in the attitude of walking. The president then proceeds to ask the following questions of the man: 'Do you, brother (calling him by name), take sister (calling the bride by name) by the right hand, to receive her unto yourself, to be your lawful and wedded wife, and you to be her lawful and wedded husband, for time and for all eternity, with a covenant and promise on your part that you will fulfil all the laws, rites, and ordinances pertaining to this holy matrimony, in the new and everlasting covenant—doing this in the presence of God, angels, and these witnesses, of your own free will and choice?' The bridegroom answers, 'Yes.' The president then puts the question to the bride: 'Do you, sister (calling her by name), take brother (calling him by name) by the right hand, and give yourself to him to be his lawful and wedded wife, for time and for all eternity, with a covenant and promise, on your part, that you will fulfil all the laws, rites, and ordinances pertaining to this holy matrimony, in the new and everlasting covenant—doing this in the presence of God, angels, and these witnesses, of your own free-will and choice?' The bride answers, 'Yes.' The president then says: 'In the name of the Lord Jesus Christ, and by the authority of the holy priesthood, I pronounce you legally and lawfully husband and wife, for time and all eternity; and I seal upon you the blessings of the holy resurrection, with power to come forth in the morning of the first resurrection, clothed with glory, immortality, and eternal lives; and I seal upon you the blessings of thrones, and dominions, and principalities, and powers, and exaltations; together with the blessings of Abraham, Isaac, and Jacob; and say unto you, be fruitful and multiply, and replenish the earth, that you may have joy and rejoicing in your posterity, in the day of the Lord Jesus. All these blessings, together with all other blessings pertaining to the new and everlasting covenant, I seal upon your heads, and enjoin your faithfulness unto the end, by the authority of the holy priesthood, in the name of the Father, and of the Son, and of the Holy Ghost. Amen.'"

This is the ordinary marriage ceremony, and applies, with slight variations to suit the facts, equally in cases of polygamy or monogamy. There is a higher degree in the temple mysteries, into which the favored ones are initiated, called the "Order of the Cloistered Saints," thus explained by seceding Mormons:

"When an apostle, high-priest, elder, or scribe, conceives an affection for a female, and has ascertained her views on the subject, he communicates confidentially to the prophet his love-affair, and requests him to inquire of the Lord whether or not it would be right and proper for him to take unto himself this woman for his spiritual wife. It is no obstacle whatever to this spiritual marriage, if one or both of the parties should happen to have a husband or wife already, according to the gentile laws of the land.

"The prophet puts the singular question to the Lord, and if he receive an answer in the affirmative, which is always the case when the parties are in favor with the president, the parties assemble in the lodge-room, accompanied by a duly-authorized administrator, and place themselves kneeling before the altar. The administrator commences the ceremony by saying: 'You separately and jointly, in the name of Jesus Christ, the Son of God, do solemnly covenant and agree, that you will not disclose any matter relating to the sacred act now in progress of consummation, whereby any gentile shall come to the knowledge of the secret purposes of this order, or whereby the saints may suffer persecution, your lives being the forfeit.'

"Then comes the ceremony of marriage, after which the parties leave the cloister, with, generally, a firm belief, at least on the part of the female, in the sacredness and validity of the ceremonial, and consider themselves as united in spiritual marriage, the duties and privileges of which are in no particular different from those of any other marriage covenant."

Extended particulars of this ceremony have been disclosed, which may and may not be literally true, for none but initiates are supposed to be qualified fully to unveil the secrets of the cloister; but it is believed the foregoing will suffice for the reader. This spiritual wifeism is held to be a very solemn affair by the Mormon dignitaries. The bride-saint may have another husband, and if he happen to be a gentile, it is deemed quite essential that the "sealing" be performed in this sworn manner. The women thus entrapped are generally young and ignorant, and made to believe that their salvation depends on embracing this Mormon doctrine.

President Young usually officiates on these occasions, though Kimball, the second in the presidency, and also such of the bishops as may from time to time be commissioned by the prophet, are permitted to perform these marriage services. Divorces are of frequent occurrence, granted only by Young; and this is supposed to be a good source of revenue, the lowest fee being ten dollars. And no man is allowed to leave his wife or wives without a divorce.

"How do the Mormon women like and bear polygamy?" Mr. Bowles, upon knowledge derived from personal observation and interviews with the people concerned, answers this question:

"The universal testimony of all but their husbands is, that it is a grievous sorrow and burden; only cheerfully submitted to and embraced under a religious fanaticism and self-abnegation rare to behold, and possible only to women. They are taught to believe, and many of them really do believe, that through and by it they secure a higher and more glorious reward in the future world. 'Lord Jesus has laid a heavy trial upon me,' said one poor woman, 'but I mean to bear it for His sake, and for the glory He will grant me in His kingdom.' This is the common wail, the common solace. Such are the teachings of the Church; and I have no doubt both husbands and wives alike often honestly accept this view of the odious practice, and seek and submit to polygamy as really God's holy service, calculated to make saints of themselves and all associated with them in the future world.

"In some cases they live harmoniously and lovingly together; oftener, it would seem, they have separate parts of the same house, or even separate houses. The first wife is generally the recognized one of society, and frequently assumes contempt for the others, regarding them as concubines, and not wives. But it is a dreadful state of society to any one of fine feelings and true instincts; it robs married life of all its sweet sentiment and companionship; and while it degrades woman, it brutalizes man, teaching him to despise and domineer over his wives, over all women. It breeds jealousy, distrust, and tempts to infidelity; but the police system of the Church and the community is so strict and constant, that it is claimed and believed the latter vice is very rare. The effect upon the children cannot help being debasing, however well they may be guarded and educated."

The tithing system is the great support of the Church and of its rulers. It was the main source of the wealth that had been accumulated by Smith at the period of his death; his successor has doubtless largely exceeded him in this particular. The original tithing revelation by Smith has been modified and strengthened by Young. Every adult immigrant or new-comer joining the Church, is expected to pay one-tenth of his or her entire possessions, and careful inventories of their whole property of every kind are made for this purpose, by a bishop and clerk from the tithing-office. This levy is paid in cash when possible. The penalty for non-payment is exclusion from the Church and from all spiritual blessings.

An immigrant fund is founded for the aid of "saints" coming to the new Jerusalem from foreign countries, which is made up by the tithing system. A fixed tariff of rates is observed in the tithe levies upon all new converts, and also upon members of the Church in Utah desirous to be joined by their friends abroad. This fund is under the exclusive control of the great autocrat of Salt Lake; and it is supposed to be another fruitful source of his personal revenue. Terrible hardships, not previously dreamed of by immigrants, are often endured by them in their journey across the plains—so that they are apt to be quite content with their new Mormon home when they reach it; and it is then too late to change their destiny, if they wish to do so.

The Mormons have an organized militia, of which Young assumes the command, as "Governor of the State of Deseret." The Nauvoo Legion, an independent battalion first raised by Smith in Illinois, is attached to the same general command. Though, as has been seen, these forces have on several occasions been called to meet detachments of the army of the United States, no actual collision has at any time occurred. Young fights valiantly in his "sermons," but is careful to avoid the disagreeable odor of constitutional gunpowder. General Conner is in command of the Federal forces in Utah Territory, with his headquarters at Camp Douglas.

A secret organization of desperadoes called Danites is among the institutions of Salt Lake. They are a sort of standing picket-guard, or vigilance committee; their province is to keep an espionage upon the movements of the Federal Territorial officers; and in any case requiring desperate action, the biddings of the prophet as communicated to their leader, are instantly obeyed. They are also "avenging angels," held in readiness to retaliate any offences against the Church or its president by apostates or others. Secret assassinations have been charged against them, and in fact no other explanation has ever been given for many instances of horrid murder of apostates and gentiles perpetrated in the vicinity of Salt Lake.

As the conclusion of this historic review, the "revelation" is believingly proclaimed, that the accumulating elements of self-dissolution inherent in the system of the Mormon brotherhood are certain to work out the ultimate disenthralment of the fanatic masses from the absolutism now controlling their minds and action, with the final and ignominious downfall of the imposture theocracy. And is it an irrational "prophecy," that such termination of its abominations and criminalities will not much longer be procrastinated, by any means short of another "martyrdom" or the cementing influences of some similar intervention for the preservation of the guilty sect profaning the name of religion? that the point of time will soon be reached, when the Great Jehovah shall pronounce the irrevocable fiat to the Mormon impostors, "Thus far shalt thou come, but no farther—and here shall thy proud waves be stayed"?

APPENDIX.

LETTER OF HON. STEPHEN S. HARDING, LATE GOVERNOR OF UTAH TERRITORY.

MILAN, INDIANA, *June* 1, 1867.

POMEROY TUCKER, ESQ. :

MY DEAR SIR,—Your letter of 22d was received on my coming home from court last night. I entirely approve your plan of Mormon history, beginning as you do with its origin in the illusory tricks of Joe Smith, which he had practised upon his superstitious followers for years anterior to his Golden Bible "vision," and before he had dreamed of becoming a "prophet." I knew Smith, and also Martin Harris and Oliver Cowdery, with some of their fanatical associates at and around Palmyra, and heard much of their early delusions, and can appreciate the importance to the civilized world of your forthcoming narrative. It has long been needed to complete the history of Latter-Day Saintism, and it has been a matter of wonder to me that such a disclosure of the great pretension, showing the nothingness of its groundwork, was not written up years ago. With your facilities for performing this service—your personal knowledge of the whole imposture and its authors—you cannot fail in producing a work of general interest and popular favor. I will proceed at once to answer your inquiries so far as I can.

PARLEY P. PRATT.

This important character in the origin of the Mormon Church was assassinated in Arkansas, in 1856 or '57, by the enraged husband of a woman who had been converted by the missionary labors of the victim, while they were attempting flight to Salt Lake. I believe the assassin was acquitted on some preliminary investigation, and his "converted" wife was permitted to pursue her journey to Salt Lake, where she is now living with the "saints." She left several children, as well as her husband, at her forsaken home. Orson Pratt, a brother of the deceased, is among the leading men of the Mormon Church, and is accepted as second in scholarship to none in the brotherhood.

THE TEMPLE PROJECT.

I cannot tell you the exact dimensions of the proposed temple. It is immense in its plan, on paper, but will probably never be built. The foundation is laid, and that is about all that has been done upon the structure, though the *tithing* for this "great work of the Lord" is not neglected. The basement or foundation-walls are eighteen feet high and twelve feet thick, composed of dressed stone in heavy blocks. Should the temple ever be completed according to the original design, it would be the most massive church edifice on this continent, perhaps not inferior to St. Peter's of Rome.

PLACES OF MORMON WORSHIP.

The two principal places of worship are within the Temple Block, consisting of the Tabernacle, a large structure used in the inclement seasons, and the Bowery, which is a canopy made of the boughs of trees, ample for the seating of five or six thousand people. The semi-annual conferences, in the spring and fall, are held in the Bowery. I have often seen every inch of the room in this vast amphitheatre packed with human beings, with eager eyes turned to the sacred platform, where "Brother Brigham" and the other high functionaries of the Mormon hierarchy utter their fulminations against the unrepentant gentile world. With all this, there is really excellent music—a full choir of well-trained singers of both sexes—accompanied by a first-class band of wind and string instruments. The scene is sometimes indescribably grand in a theatrical sense. Young evidently knows and *feels* the strength of his power over his vast body of worshippers.

POPULATION OF THE CITY AND TERRITORY.

The population of Utah at this time must be over one hundred thousand—the number of Mormons alone cannot fall far short of that figure. Great Salt Lake City now contains nearly or quite twenty thousand souls. The gentiles in the Territory probably number two thousand. When I first arrived in Utah, in 1863, there was not more than one gentile to one thousand Mormons. I am unable to answer your question how many Mormons there are "in all creation," but I have heard it announced in a seemingly boastful spirit, on the stands at the Tabernacle and the Bowery, that there were five hundred thousand "saints" in Europe, and that the numbers were continually increasing by the instrumentality of the missionary labors. Probably a million is a reasonable estimate for the whole number of converts from the beginning, including those who have apostatized.

THE CHURCH AND POLYGAMY.

The Church of Latter-Day Saints is believed to be the most powerful organization, religious or political, that has been founded in modern history. Its absolutism is complete and crushing. The people are peculiarly industrious and temperate in their habits—owing, probably, in a large degree to the fact that in the first settlement of the country they were required to work or perish, thus early contracting the habits that distinguish their community. Polygamy is not universal in Mormon households, the question being left to individual choice, rather than to any compulsory Church dogma. It is chiefly among the official and aspiring members of the Church and the "well-to-do" "saints," that the plural-wife system is adopted. As a general thing the Mormon women condemn it, including those connected with its practice, as well as the more positive resistants of "the faith."

THE PROPHET'S TITHING RESOURCES.

Young possesses extraordinary executive abilities. In the name of the temple and other public enterprises, his tithing exactions are enforced with unvarying strictness, and with little if any visible murmuring among those who bear the burden. Every thing is subject to the system, from the tenth egg to the tenth horse, and from the tenth cent to the tenth dollar—the poor girl who works out by the week, and the rich farmer or money-lender, being indiscriminately subject to this tithe levy "in the Lord's name." All these resources go into Brother Brigham's hands, and he is never required to make a report or exhibit a balance-sheet to his disciples. He has thus received millions upon millions of money, besides untold amounts in property values of every description. Is it any wonder that his private coffers are ample for the affluent maintenance of his sixty wives and one hundred and fifty children, more or less?

PIONEER MORMONS—SACRED RELIC.

When I was in Palmyra in 1829, I went with Joe Smith, at his special request, to his father's house, in company with Martin Harris and Oliver Cowdery, for the purpose of hearing read his wonderful "translations" from the sacred plates. This was before these revelations had been given to the world in the printed "Book of Mormon." Subsequently, after the printing contract had been concluded between Grandin and Harris, I was in the printing-office with yourself, and also the three pioneer Mormons named, when the proof-sheet of the first form of the book, including the title-page, was revised by you. A corrected impression of it was passed around to the young prophet and his attendant disciples, all of whom appeared to be delighted with the dawning of the new gospel dispensation, and it was accepted by Smith as "according to revelation." By consent of the brotherhood, you finally gave this "revise sheet" to me as a curiosity, and I retained it until some two years after Smith's murder, and before the Mormons had gone to Utah, when it was bestowed by me upon a grateful wandering "saint" of the name of Robert Campbell, who had been cared for over night at my present residence. This "sacred relic" is now among the archives in the "Historian's Office" at Salt Lake City.

COMMAND TO PREACH THE MORMON GOSPEL.

You ask me to write my recollections of the "call" to preach the Mormon gospel, as "revealed" to Calvin Stoddard in 1829. I can do so with as distinct a remembrance as if that unjustifiable act of a "wild and fast young man" had occurred yesterday. I can never forget it, for I was almost as badly scared, before I had got done with the mischief, as poor Calvin was; and I have never to this day been quite satisfied with my conduct. I was especially led to play the trick by the strange credulity which Martin Harris had manifested the same day, as we walked together to hear Lorenzo Dow preach in Palmyra. Added to this inducement, Calvin had previously told me of the wonderful things he had seen in the sky, and of his serious impressions about his duty to preach the new gospel. My purpose was to try an experiment in delusion, upon Joe Smith's principle, merely for my own amusement and instruction. The main story is the same as you have related it in the extract of your manuscript sent me, and it need not be repeated in this letter. . . . . I remained at the door only for a moment, long enough to hear the startled Mormon saint in his fright cry out to his Maker in supplication for mercy and promise of obedience; when, taking to my heels, no young scapegrace ever did *taller running*, in proportion to locomotive capacity, than I did that dark night. I was stopping for a few days as a guest with my relative, Mr. Hill, in the vicinity, and gained access to my room about eleven o'clock without discovery. . . . . Pale and haggard in appearance, from lack of sleep or perhaps from repentance for his former disobedience, Stoddard was early the next morning in the fulfilment of the "command" among his neighbors, relating in the most earnest manner the marvellous particulars of the miracle of which he was the "chosen" subject. He repeated the words of the "celestial messenger" as addressed to him, with entire accuracy, and said they were communicated amid the roaring thunders of heaven and the musical sounds of angels' wings. For aught I have ever heard since, he held out to the end faithful to his ministerial calling in the Mormon cause. Sincerely regretting my mischievous experiment—for I really began to feel conscientious qualms about it—I sought to relieve my fanatic friend of his delusion, by the suggestion that probably some unprincipled person had imposed upon him, advising him to give no heed to the trick; but I found that no such theory could be made available for my well-intended purpose, for he had "spiritual" evidences on the subject that were above any human testimony! . . . . Poor Stoddard has gone to his final account. Peace to his ashes! If that thoughtless act of my boyhood, thirty-eight years ago, caused him one hour's unhappiness, or contributed in any degree to a single conversion to Mormonism, may He who "tempers the wind to the shorn lamb" look upon my offence not in anger, but in mercy, for I know that I did not intend to do a premeditated wrong to any one.

Truly yours,

STEPHEN S. HARDING.

STATEMENT OF THE LATE REV. JESSE TOWNSEND.

For the following sketch of the origin of the Mormon imposture, and of its leader "Joe Smith" and his early associates and dupes, the author of this work is indebted to the kindness of Mrs. Perrine, daughter of the writer, the late Rev. Jesse Townsend. It is the original manuscript of a letter written at its date, by Mr. Townsend, in answer to inquiries for information addressed to him by Mr. Phineas Stiles, of Wendell, Franklin County, Massachusetts, in November, 1833, who set forth that two men from Ohio were actively engaged in his town and vicinity, and with an alarming degree of success, in efforts to disseminate among the people and in the churches, "a new revelation and a new religion, which they call the Mormon religion," and that they "pretend to be inspired and empowered by God to teach" the same. This statement of Mr. Townsend, made soon after the Mormon advent, now first published, may be regarded as a further important authentication of the foregoing pioneer history of the sect of people now become so prosperous and powerful in Utah Territory.

PALMYRA, WAYNE COUNTY, N. Y., *December* 24, 1833.

MR. PHINEAS STILES:

DEAR SIR,—Your letter of 29th ultimo, requesting information concerning the class of people called Mormonites, has been received, and the following is a sketch of their history:

This new sect was commenced by Joseph Smith, Jr., in the vicinity of this village some four years ago, and the statement I give you is the *truth*, incredible as it may appear to you, and shows the folly and weakness of the people who have listened to and heeded the impositions and falsehoods propagated by Smith and his associates in iniquity.

I begin with the leader, "Joe," as he is and always has been called here. For the ten years I have known any thing of him, he has been a person of questionable character, of intemperate habits, and latterly a noted *money-digger*. He lived in a sequestered neighborhood, where, with his dupes, his impostures and low cunning gave him a reputation for being "smart." He has had a stone, into which, when placed in a hat, he pretended to look and see chests of money buried in the earth. He was also a *fortune-teller*, and he claimed to know where stolen goods went—probably too well.

Smith flattered a few of his peculiar fraternity to engage with him in digging for money. After a while, many of these got out of patience with his false pretensions and repeated failures; and, finally, to avoid the sneers of those who had been deceived by him, he pretended that he had found, in digging alone, a wonderful curiosity, which he kept closely secreted. After telling different stories about it, and applying to it different names, he at length called it *the golden plates of the Book of Mormon.* As he was questioned on the subject from time to time, his story assumed a more uniform statement, the term finally given to the marvellous treasure being the "Golden Bible."

In the mean time, Joe visited a visionary fanatic by the name of Martin Harris, and told him he had received some golden plates of ancient records from the Lord, with a "revelation" to call on him for fifty dollars to enable him to go to Pennsylvania and translate the contents of the plates; at the same time telling Harris that the Lord had revealed to him that they (Smith and Harris) were the only honest men in the world. This at once took with the dupe, who had specially prided himself on his honesty; and the wily deceiver understood this fact; he knew this was the assailable point in his victim's visionary mind. The delicious bait was greedily swallowed; and the fifty dollars was soon put into the hands of Smith, who cleared for Pennsylvania or elsewhere.

At that time Martin Harris was worth five or six thousand dollars, while the Smiths were not worth a cent. The latter used Martin's money freely; and some other men, having a great dislike to labor, joined Joe in his deceptions, among whom was a sort of schoolmaster named Cowdery, who assisted him in writing or transcribing the "Book of Mormon," as a pretended translation of the golden plates which he affirmed he had been directed by the Spirit of the Lord to dig from the earth. This was all done in the most secret manner. At the same time it was assumed to the uninitiated that it would be "immediate death" for any except the translators to see the plates. Poor Martin's faith was apparently strengthened by this pretension, but afterward the "command" was modified, and he claimed to have seen the plates with "spiritual eyes."*

This Harris, who is or has been second in authority among the Mormonites, was an industrious farmer, living near this village, who had been unfortunate in the choice of a wife, or she had been in that of a husband. Like his leader, he gives to their preachers the power to preach and put their proselytes under water by authority of the new "revelation." He has whipped his wife and beaten her so cruelly and frequently, that she was obliged to seek refuge in separation. . . . . He is considered here, to this day, a brute in his domestic relations, a fool and dupe to Smith in religion, and an unlearned, conceited hypocrite, generally. He paid for printing the Book of Mormon, which exhausted all his money and most of his property. Since he went to Ohio he has attempted to get another wife, though it is believed he was frustrated in this design by the discovery of his having a living wife here.

All the Mormonites have left this part of our State, and so palpable is their imposture that nothing is here said or thought of the subject, except when inquiries from abroad are occasionally made concerning them. I know of no one now living in this section of country that ever gave them credence. Joe Smith dare not come to Palmyra, from fear

* Mr. Townsend, at the date of his letter, had not learned of the connection of Rigdon and the Spaulding manuscript with this matter.

of his creditors; for he ran away to avoid their just demands.

You, sir, may think we treat this matter lightly; but I give you a correct statement. You have asked for the facts, and I give them. We consider the founders and propagators of the Mormon "religion" simply as base impostors, whose sectarian assertions are false and absurd.

Respectfully yours, etc.,

JESSE TOWNSEND.

WAR ROMANCE OF MORMONISM.

ACCORDING to the Mormon fable—*alias* the Spaulding romance or Joe Smith revelation—the people inhabiting our American continent in its wilderness state were very warlike tribes, especially the Nephites and Lamanites (see chapter viii.) A melancholy history of their military and spiritual dealings is presented in the following brief collection from different books of the "Book of Mormon," which will repay perusal by the admirer of the marvellous, whether he accept the narrative in the light of fiction or fact:

EXTRACTS FROM THE BOOK OF MORMON.

"And now it came to pass that I, Enos, went about among the people of Nephi, prophesying of things to come, and testifying of the things which I had heard and seen. And I bare record that the people of Nephi did seek diligently to restore the Lamanites unto the true faith in God. But our labors were vain; their hatred was fixed, and they were led by their evil nature, that they became wild and ferocious, and a bloodthirsty people; full of idolatry and filthiness; feeding upon beasts of prey, dwelling in tents, and wandering about in the wilderness, with a short skin girded about their loins, and their heads shaven; and their skill was in the bow, and the cimeter, and the axe. And many of them did eat nothing save it was raw meat; and they were continually seeking to destroy us.

"And it came to pass that the people of Nephi did till the land, and raise all manner of grain, and of fruit, and flocks of herds, and flocks of all manner of cattle, of every kind, and goats, and wild goats, and also much horses. And there were exceeding many prophets among us. And the people were a stiff-necked people, hard to understand. And I saw wars between the Nephites and the Lamanites in the course of my days. And it came to pass that I began to be old, and an hundred and seventy-and-nine years had passed away from the time that our father Lehi left Jerusalem. And as I saw that I must soon go down to my grave, having been wrought upon by the power of God, that I must preach and prophesy unto this people, and declare the word according to the truth which is in Christ."—*Book of Enos.*

"And now, behold, two hundred years had passed away, and the people of Nephi had waxed strong in the land. They observed to keep the law of Moses and the Sabbath-day holy unto the Lord. And they profaned not; neither did they blaspheme. And the laws of the land were exceeding strict. And they were scattered upon much of the face of the land, and the Lamanites also. And they were exceeding more numerous than were they of the Nephites; and they loved murder, and would drink the blood of beasts.

"And it came to pass that they came many times against us, the Nephites, to battle. But our kings and our leaders were mighty men in the faith of the Lord; and they taught the people the ways of the Lord; wherefore, we withstood the Lamanites, and swept them away out of our lands, and began to fortify our cities, or whatsoever place of our inheritance. And we multiplied exceedingly and spread upon the face of the land, and became exceeding rich in gold, and in silver, and in precious things, and in fine workmanship of wood, in buildings, and in machinery, and also in iron, and copper, and brass, and steel, making all manner of tools of every kind to till the ground, and weapons of war; yea, the sharp-pointed arrow, and the quiver, and the dart, and the javelin, and all preparations for war; and thus being prepared to meet the Lamanites, they did not prosper against us."—*Book of Jarom.*

"I, Zeniff, having been taught in all the language of the Nephites, and having had a knowledge of the land of Nephi, or of the land of our fathers' first inheritance, and I having been sent as a spy among the Lamanites, that I might spy out their forces, that our army might come upon them and destroy them; but when I saw that which was good among them, I was desirous that they should not be destroyed; therefore I contended with my brethren in the wilderness: for I would that our ruler should make a treaty with them. But he, being an austere and a bloodthirsty man, commanded that I should be slain; but I was rescued by the shedding of much blood, for father fought against father, and brother against brother, until the greatest number of our army was destroyed in the wilderness; and we returned, those of us that were spared, to the land of Zarahemla, to relate that tale to their wives and their children. And yet, I being over-zealous to inherit the land of our fathers, collected as many as were desirous to go up to possess the land, and started again on our journey into the wilderness to go up to the land; but we were smitten with famine and sore afflictions: for we were slow to remember the Lord our God. . . .

"And it came to pass that I did arm them with bows, and with arrows, with swords, and with cimeters, and with clubs, and with slings, and with all manner of weapons which we could invent, and I and my people did go forth against the Lamanites to battle; yea, in the strength of the Lord did we go forth to battle against the Lamanites: for I and my people did cry mightily to the Lord that he would deliver us out of the hands of our enemies, for we were awakened to a remembrance of the deliverance of our fathers. And God did hear our cries, and did answer our prayers; and we did go forth in his might. Yea, we did go forth against the Lamanites; and in one day and a night we did slay three thousand and forty-three; we did slay them, even until we had driven them out of our land. And I, myself, with mine own hands, did help to bury their dead. And behold, to our great sorrow and lamentation, two hundred and seventy-nine of our brethren were slain."—*Book of Mosiah.*

"And it came to pass that the Lamanites made preparations for war, and came up to the land of Nephi for the purpose of destroying the king and to place another in his stead, and also of destroying the people of anti-Nephi-Lehi out of the land. And it came to pass that when the people saw that they were coming against them, they went out to meet them, and prostrated themselves before them to the earth, and began to call on the name of the Lord; and thus they were in this attitude when the Lamanites began to fall upon them, and began to slay them with the sword; and thus, without meeting any resistance, they did slay a thousand and five of them; and we know that they are blessed, for they have gone to dwell with their God. Now when the Lamanites saw that their brethren would not flee from the sword, neither would they turn aside to the right hand or to the left, but that they would lay down and perish, and praised God even in the very act of perishing under the sword; now when the Lamanites saw this, they did forbear from slaying them; and there were many whose hearts had swollen in them for those of their brethren who had fallen under the sword, for they repented of the things which they had done. . . . .

"And now it came to pass that after the people of Ammon were established in the land of Jershon, and a Church also established in the land of Jershon; and the armies of the Nephites were set round about the land of Jershon; yea, in all the borders round about the land of Zarahemla; behold, the armies of the Lamanites had followed their brethren into the wilderness. And thus a tremendous battle: yea, even such an one as never had been known among all the people in the land from the time that Lehi left Jerusalem; yea, and tens of thousands of the Lamanites were slain and scattered abroad. Yea, and also there was a tremendous slaughter among the people of Nephi; nevertheless, the Lamanites were driven and scattered, and the people of Nephi returned again to their land. . . . .

"And it came to pass that the Lamanites came up on the north of the hill where a part of the army of Moroni was concealed. And as the Lamanites had passed the hill Replah, and came into the valley, and began to cross the river Sidon, the army which was concealed on the south of the hill, which was led by a man whose name was Lehi; and he led his army forth and encircled the Lamanites about on the east, in their rear.

"And it came to pass that the Lamanites, when they saw the Nephites coming upon them in their rear, turned them about, and began to contend with the army of Lehi; and the work of death commenced on both sides; but it was more dreadful on the part of the Lamanites; for their nakedness was exposed to the heavy blows of the Nephites with their swords and their cimeters, which brought death almost at every stroke; while on the other hand there was now and then a man fell among the Nephites by their swords and the loss of blood; they being shielded at the more vital parts of the body, or the more vital parts of the body being shielded from the strokes of the Lamanites by their breastplates, and their arm-shields, and their head-plates; and thus the Nephites did carry on the work of death among the Lamanites."—*Book of Alma.*

"And there was a great famine upon the land, among all the people of Nephi. And thus, in the seventy-and-fourth year, the famine did continue, and the work of destruction did cease by the sword, but became sore by famine. And this work of destruction did also continue in the seventy-and-fifth year. For the earth was smitten, that it was dry, and did not yield forth grain in the season of grain; and the whole earth was smitten, even among the Lamanites as well as among the Nephites, so that they were smitten that they did perish by thousands in the more wicked parts of the land."—*Book of Helaman.*

"And now I finish my record concerning the destruction of my people, the Nephites. And it came to pass that we did march forth before the Lamanites. And I, Mormon, wrote an epistle unto the king of the Lamanites, and desired of him that he would grant unto us that we might gather together our people unto the land of Camorah, by a hill which was called Camorah, and there we would give them battle. . . . .

"And it came to pass that my people, with their wives and their children, did now behold the armies of the Lamanites marching toward them; and with that awful fear of death which fills the breasts of all the wicked, did they await to receive them. And it came to pass that they came to battle against us, and every soul was filled with terror because of the greatness of their numbers. And it came to pass that they did fall upon my people with the sword, and with the bow, and with the arrow, and with the axe, and with all manner of weapons of war. And it came to pass that my men were hewn down, yea, even my ten thousand which were with me, and I fell wounded in the midst; and they passed by me that they did not put an end to my life. And when they had gone through and hewn down all my people save it were twenty-and-four of us (among whom was my son Moroni), and we having survived the dead of our people, did behold on the morrow, when the Lamanites had returned unto their camps, from the top of the hill Camorah, the ten thousand of my people which were hewn down, being led in the front by me; and we also beheld the ten thousand of my people which were led by my son Moroni. And behold, the ten thousand of Gidgiddonah had fallen, and he also in the midst; and Lamah had fallen with his ten thousand; and Gilgal had fallen with his ten thousand; and Limhah had fallen with his ten thousand; and Joneam had fallen with his ten thousand; and Camenihah, and Moronihah, and Antionum, and Shiblom, and Shem, and Josh, had fallen with their ten thousand each."—*Book of Mormon.*

"Now there began to be a war upon all the face of the land, every man with his band, fighting for that which he desired. And there were robbers, and, in fine, all manner of wickedness upon all the face of the land. And it came to pass that Coriantumr was exceeding angry with Shared, and he went against him with his armies to battle; and they did meet in great anger; and they did meet in the valley of Gilgal; and the battle became exceeding sore. And it came to pass that Shared fought against him for the space of three days. And it came to pass that Coriantumr beat him, and did pursue him until he came to the plains of Heshlon. And it came to pass that Shared gave him battle again upon the plains; and behold, he did beat Coriantumr, and drove him back again to the valley of Gilgal. And Coriantumr gave Shared battle again in the valley of Gilgal, in the which he beat Shared, and slew him. And Shared wounded Coriantumr in his thigh, that he did not go to battle again for the space of two years, in the which time all the people upon all the face of the land were shedding blood, and there was none to constrain them. . . . .

" And the battle became exceeding sore, and many thousands fell by the sword. And it came to pass that Coriantumr did lay siege to the wilderness, and the brother of Shared did march forth out of the wilderness by night, and slew a part of the army of Coriantumr, as they were drunken. And he came forth to the land of Moron, and placed himself upon the throne of Coriantumr. And it came to pass that Coriantumr dwelt with his army in the wilderness for the space of two years, in the which he did receive great strength to his army. And it came to pass that one of the secret combinations murdered him in a secret pass, and obtained unto himself the kingdom; and his name was Lib; and Lib was a man of great stature, more than any other man among all the people. . . . .

" Now the name of the brother of Lib was called Shiz. And Shiz pursued after Coriantumr, and he did overthrow many cities, and he did slay both women and children, and he did burn the cities thereof; and there went a fear of Shiz throughout all the land; yea, a cry went forth throughout the land: Who can stand before the army of Shiz? Behold, he sweepeth the earth before him! . . . .

" And so great and lasting had been the war, and so long had been the scene of bloodshed and carnage, that the whole face of the land was covered with the bodies of the dead; and so swift and speedy was the war that there was none left to bury the dead; but they did march forth from the shedding of blood to the shedding of blood, leaving the bodies of men, women, and children, strewn upon the face of the land, to become a prey to the worms of the flesh; and the scent thereof went forth upon the face of the land, even upon all the face of the land; wherefore the people became troubled by day and by night, because of the scent thereof; nevertheless, Shiz did not cease to pursue Coriantumr, for he had sworn to avenge himself upon Coriantumr of the blood of his brother which had been slain, and the word of the Lord which came to Ether, that Coriantumr should not fall by the sword. And thus we see that the Lord did visit them in the fulness of his wrath, and their wickedness and abominations had prepared a way for their everlasting destruction."—*Book of Ether.*

INSTITUTIONS OF THE MORMON METROPOLIS.

New Tabernacle Completed—The great Unfinished Temple—Young's Theory of Christ's Second Coming, etc.

A NEW Tabernacle, commenced by the Latter-Day Saints in 1862, has just been completed and dedicated to the Mormon service at Salt Lake City. It is a large adobe edifice, plain in its architecture, and computed to be ample for the accommodation of eight thousand Mormons. This structure supplies the place of the old Tabernacle (or Endowment-House), and the Bowery. It stands inside the walls enclosing the immense area called "Temple Block."

The adobes used in this building, with suitable foundation and coping, are found on trial to be substantial and durable in a climate like that of Utah. They are made of a peculiar kind of blue clay abounding in the Territory, similar in shape to common brick, though larger, being sun-dried instead of kiln-burnt. The theatre, penitentiary, and most of the buildings of the city, are constructed of these adobes.

The great unfinished "Temple of the Lord" is a magnificent *project;* but beyond the erection of its massive foundation walls it is little more than a project. So far as progressed, the building is composed of huge blocks of granite, hewn from the quarry at Cottonwood Cañon, and hauled by ox-teams a distance of eighteen miles. An eye-witness writes: "One of these blocks generally makes a load for ten or twelve oxen, and three days are spent in delivering each load. Contemplate for a moment the character and amount of labor performed—the innumerable tons of wrought granite required—and ask yourself, at what age of the world has like obedience to 'spiritual authority' been yielded without compensation since the building of the pyramids of Cheops and Ghizeh? For, it is to be remembered that all this work is done in *commutation of tithes.* And then calculate, if you can, the probabilities in regard to the period of the future when the monster temple, to contain eighteen thousand Mormon saints, is to receive its finishing stone!"

The theory inculcated by Young, and disseminated by his apostles and priesthood, and probably believed by their deluded followers, is, that he is to experience great mortal longevity; that Christ, at his second coming, is to be his ultimate successor; and that this event will occur when the "saints" shall have finished the building of a temple suitable for the Saviour's reception, and not before. His language, as uttered from the pulpit, and literally reported, is: "When the temple is completed—that very day—yes, that very hour—Christ, with his holy angels, and the prophets and apostles, and Joseph and Hyrum (meaning the Smiths), and all the saints who have died in the faith, and all who have obeyed revealed authority, will come to set up His kingdom on earth."

Of course the arch-impostor is sharp enough to prolong his power and aggrandizement by delaying the completion of the temple for many years to come; and, in truth, at the rate of progress that has been made already, it would take a century if not centuries to finish that sacred receptacle. This artifice essentially aids in the maintenance of a prestige and dominion among his believers equal to any requirement in his own behalf.

The problem to be solved by time and events, is an interesting one for the followers of truth: When the present autocrat of Mormondom shall come to obey the inexorable fiat addressed to all living, as sooner or later he must, "Dust thou art, and unto dust shalt thou return," can a mortal successor be found who will be able to hold up the rod of power now wielded over fanaticism with a degree of success that astonishes the civilized world?

THE END.

LIST OF WORKS

PUBLISHED BY D. APPLETON & CO.,

Nos. 443 & 445 Broadway, N. Y.

A Descriptive Catalogue, with full titles and prices, may be had gratuitously on application.

About's Roman Question.
Adams' Boys at Home.
—— Edgar Clifton.
Addison's Spectator. 6 vols.
Adler's German and English Dictionary.
—— Abridged do. do. do.
—— German Reader.
—— " Literature.
—— Ollendorff for Learning German.
—— Key to the Exercises.
—— Iphigenia in Tauris.
After Icebergs with a Painter.
Agnel's Book of Chess.
Aguilar's Home Influence.
—— Mother's Recompense.
—— Days of Bruce. 2 vols.
—— Home Scenes.
—— Woman's Friendship.
—— Women of Israel. 2 vols.
—— Vale of Cedars.
Ahn's French Method.
—— Spanish Grammar.
—— A Key to same.
—— German Method. 1 vol.
Or, separately—First Course. 1 vol.
Second " 1 vol.
Aids to Faith. A series of Essays, by Various Writers.
Aikin's British Poets. From Chaucer to the Present Time. 3 vols.
Album for Postage Stamps.
Albums of Foreign Galleries; in 7 folios.
Alden's Elements of Intellectual Philosophy.
Alison's Miscellaneous Essays.
Allen's Mechanics of Nature.
Alsop's Charms of Fancy.
Amelia's Poems.
American Poets (Gems from the).
American Eloquence. A Collection of Speeches and Addresses. 2 vols.
American System of Education:
1. Hand-Book of Anglo-Saxon Root-Words.
2. Hand-Book of Anglo-Saxon Derivatives.
American System of Education:
3. Hand-Book of Engrafted Words.
Anderson's Mercantile Correspondence.
Andrews' New French Instructor.
—— A Key to the above.
Annals of San Francisco.
Antisell on Coal Oils.
Anthon's Law Student.
Appletons' New American Cyclopædia of Useful Knowledge. 16 vols.
—— Annual Cyclopædia, and Register of Important Events for 1861, '62, '63, '64, '65.
—— Cyclopædia of Biography, Foreign and American.
—— Cyclopædia of Drawing.
The same in parts:
Topographical Drawing.
Perspective and Geometrical Drawing.
Shading and Shadows.
Drawing Instruments and their Uses.
Architectural Drawing and Design.
Mechanical Drawing and Design.
—— Dictionary of Mechanics and Engineering. 2 large vols.
—— Railway Guide.
—— American Illustrated Guide Book. 1 vol.
Do. do., separately:
1. Eastern and Middle States, and British Provinces. 1 vol.
2. Southern and Western States, and the Territories. 1 vol.
—— Companion Hand-Book of Travel.
Arabian Nights' Entertainments.
Arnold's (S. G.) History of the State of Rhode Island. 2 vols.
Arnold's (Dr.) History of Rome.
—— Modern History.
Arnold's Classical Series:
—— First Latin Book.
—— First and Second Latin Book and Grammar.
—— Latin Prose Composition.
—— Cornelius Nepos.
—— First Greek Book.
—— Greek Prose Composition Book, 1.

Arnold's Greek Prose Composition Book, 2.
—— Greek Reading Book.
Arthur's (T. S.) Tired of Housekeeping.
Arthur's (W.) Successful Merchant.
At Anchor; or, A Story of our Civil War.
Atlantic Library. 7 vols. in case.
Attaché in Madrid.
Aunt Fanny's Story Book.
—— Mitten Series. 6 vols. in case.
—— Night Cap Series. 6 vols. in case.

Badois' English Grammar for Frenchmen.
—— A Key to the above.
Baine's Manual of Composition and Rhetoric.
Bakewell's Great Facts
Baldwin's Flush Times.
—— Party Leaders.
Balmanno's Pen and Pencil.
Bank Law of the United States.
Barrett's Beauty for Ashes.
Bartlett's U. S. Explorations. 2 vols.
——— Cheap edition. 2 vols. in 1.
Barwell's Good in Every Thing.
Bassnett's Theory of Storms.
Baxley's West Coast of America and Hawaiian Islands.
Beach's Pelayo. An Epic.
Beall (John Y.), Trial of.
Beauties of Sacred Literature.
Beauties of Sacred Poetry.
Beaumont and Fletcher's Works. 2 vols.
Belem's Spanish Phrase Book.
Bello's Spanish Grammar (in Spanish).
Benedict's Run Through Europe.
Benton on the Dred Scott Case.
—— Thirty Years' View. 2 vols.
—— Debates of Congress. 16 vols.
Bertha Percy. By Margaret Field. 12mo.
Bertram's Harvest of the Sea. Economic and Natural History of Fishes.
Bessie and Jessie's Second Book.
Beza's Novum Testamentum.
Bibles in all styles of bindings and various prices.
Bible Stories, in Bible Language.
Black's General Atlas of the World.
Bloomfield's Farmer's Boy.
Blot's What to Eat, and How to Cook it.
Blue and Gold Poets. 6 vols. in case.
Boise's Greek Exercises.
—— First Three Books of Xenophon's Anabasis.
Bojesen's Greek and Roman Antiquities.
Book of Common Prayer. Various prices.
Boone's Life and Adventures.
Bourne's Catechism of the Steam Engine.
—— Hand-Book of the Steam Engine.
—— Treatise on the Steam Engine.
Boy's Book of Modern Travel.
—— Own Toy Maker
Bradford's Peter the Great.
Bradley's (Mary E.) Douglass Farm.
Bradley's (Chas.) Sermons.
Brady's Christmas Dream.
Breakfast, Dinner, and Tea.
British Poets. From Chaucer to the Present Time. 8 large vols.
British Poets. Cabinet Edition. 15 vols.
Brooks' Ballads and Translations.
Brown, Jones, and Robinson's Tour.
Bryan's English Grammar for Germans.
Bryant & Stratton's Commercial Law.
Bryant's Poems, Illustrated.
—— Poems. 2 vols.
—— Thirty Poems.
—— Poems. Blue and Gold.
—— Letters from Spain.
Buchanan's Administration.
Buckle's Civilization in England. 2 vols.
—— Essays.
Bunyan's Divine Emblems.
Burdett's Chances and Changes.
—— Never Too Late.
Burgess' Photograph Manual. 12mo.
Burnett (James R.) on the Thirty-nine Articles.
Burnett (Peter H.), The Path which led a Protestant Lawyer to the Catholic Church.
Burnouf's Gramatica Latina.
Burns' (Jabez) Cyclopædia of Sermons.
Burns' (Robert) Poems.
Burton's Cyclopædia of Wit and Humor. 2 vols.
Butler's Martin Van Buren.
Butler's (F.) Spanish Teacher.
Butler's (S.) Hudibras.
Butler's (T. B.) Guide to the Weather.
Butler's (Wm. Allen) Two Millions.
Byron Gallery. The Gallery of Byron Beauties.
—— Poetical Works.
—— Life and Letters.
—— Works. Illustrated.

Cœleb's Laws and Practice of Whist.
Cæsar's Commentaries.
Caird's Prairie Farming.
Calhoun's Works and Speeches. 6 vols.
Campbell's (Thos.) Gertrude of Wyoming.
—— Poems.
Campbell (Judge) on Shakespeare.
Canot, Life of Captain.
Carlyle's (Thomas) Essays.
Carreno's Manual of Politeness.

Carreno's Compendio del Manual de Urbanidad.
Casseday's Poetic Lacon.
Cavendish's Laws of Whist.
Cervantes' Don Quixote, in Spanish.
—— Don Quixote, in English.
César L'Histoire de Jules. par S. M. I. Napoleon III. Vol. I., with Maps and Portrait. (French.)
Cheap Edition, without Maps and Portrait.
Maps and Portrait, for cheap edition, in envelopes.
Champlin's English Grammar.
—— Greek Grammar.
Chase on the Constitution and Canons.
Chaucer's Poems.
Chevalier on Gold.
Children's Holidays.
Child's First History.
Choquet's French Composition.
—— French Conversation.
Cicero de Officiis.
Chittenden's Report of the Peace Convention.
—— Select Orations.
Clarke's (D. S.) Scripture Promises.
Clarke's (Mrs. Cowden) Iron Cousin.
Clark's (H. J.) Mind in Nature.
Cleaveland and Backus' Villas and Cottages.
Cleveland's (H. W. S.) Hints to Riflemen.
Cloud Crystals. A Snow Flake Album.
Cobb's (J. B.) Miscellanies.
Coe's Spanish Drawing Cards. 10 parts.
Coe's Drawing Cards. 10 parts.
Colenso on the Pentateuch. 2 vols.
—— On the Romans.
Coleridge's Poems.
Collins' Amoor.
Collins' (T. W.) Humanics.
Collet's Dramatic French Reader.
Comings' Physiology.
—— Companion to Physiology.
Comment on Parle a Paris.
Congreve's Comedy.
Continental Library. 6 vols. in case.
Cooke's Life of Stonewall Jackson.
Cookery, by an American Lady.
Cooley's Cyclopædia of Receipts.
Cooper's Mount Vernon.
Copley's Early Friendship.
—— Poplar Grove.
Cornell's First Steps in Geography.
—— Primary Geography.
—— Intermediate Geography.
—— Grammar School Geography.
—— High School Geography and Atlas.
—— High School Geography.
—— " " Atlas.
—— Map Drawing. 12 maps in case.
—— Outline Maps, with Key. 13 maps in portfolio.
—— Or, the Key, separately.
Cornwall on Music.
Correlation and Conservation of Forces.
Cortez' Life and Adventures.
Cotter on the Mass and Rubrics.
Cottin's Elizabeth; or, the Exiles of Siberia.
Cousin Alice's Juveniles.
Cousin Carrie's Sun Rays.
—— Keep a Good Heart.
Cousin's Modern Philosophy. 2 vols.
—— On the True and Beautiful.
—— Only Romance.
Coutan's French Poetry.
Covell's English Grammar.
Cowles' Exchange Tables.
Cowper's Homer's Iliad.
—— Poems.
Cox's Eight Years in Congress, from 1857 to 1865.
Coxe's Christian Ballads.
Creasy on the English Constitution.
Crisis (The).
Crosby's (A.) Geometry.
Crosby's (H.) Œdipus Tyrannus.
Crosby's (W. H.) Quintus Curtius Rufus.
Crowe's Linny Lockwood.
Curry's Volunteer Book.
Cust's Invalid's Book.
Cyclopædia of Commercial and Business Anecdotes. 2 vols.

D'Abrantes' Memoires of Napoleon. 2 vols.
Dairyman's (The) Daughter.
Dana's Household Poetry.
Darwin's Origin of Species.
Dante's Poems.
Dasent's Popular Tales from the Norse.
Davenport's Christian Unity and its Recovery.
Dawson's Archaia.
De Belem's Spanish Phrase-Book.
De Fivas' Elementary French Reader.
—— Classic French Reader.
De Foe's Robinson Crusoe.
De Girardin's Marguerite.
—— Stories of an Old Maid.
De Hart on Courts Martial.
De L'Ardeche's History of Napoleon.
De Peyrac's Comment on Parle.
De Staël's Corinne, ou L'Italie.
De Veitelle's Mercantile Dictionary.
De Vere's Spanish Grammar.
Dew's Historical Digest.
Dickens's (Charles) Works. Original Illustrations. 24 vols.
Dies Iræ and Stabat Mater, bound together.
Dies Iræ, alone, and Stabat Mater, alone.
Dix's (John A.) Winter in Madeira.
—— Speeches and Addresses. 2 vols.

Dix's (Rev. M.) Lost Unity of the Christian World.
Dr. Oldham at Greystones, and his Talk there.
Doane's Works. 4 vols.
Downing's Rural Architecture.
Dryden's Poems.
Dunlap's Spirit History of Man.
Dusseldorf Gallery, Gems from the.
Dwight on the Study of Art.
Ebony Idol (The).
Ede's Management of Steel.
Edith Vaughan's Victory.
Egloffstein's Geology and Physical Geography of Mexico.
Eichhorn's German Grammar.
Elliot's Fine Work on Birds. 7 parts, or in 1 vol.
Ellsworth's Text-Book of Penmanship.
Ely's Journal.
Enfield's Indian Corn; its Value, Culture, and Uses.
Estvan's War Pictures.
Evans' History of the Shakers.
Evelyn's Life of Mrs. Godolphin.
Everett's Mount Vernon Papers.

Fables, Original and Selected.
Farrar's History of Free Thought.
Faustus.
Fay's Poems.
Fénélon's Telemaque.
——— The same, in 2 vols.
——— Telemachus.
Field's Bertha Percy.
Field's (M.) City Architecture.
Figuier's World before the Deluge.
Fireside Library. 8 vols. in case.
First Thoughts.
Fiji and the Fijians.
Flint's Physiology of Man.
Florian's William Tell.
Flower Pictures.
Fontana's Italian Grammar.
Foote's Africa and the American Flag.
Foresti's Italian Extracts.
Four Gospels (The).
Franklin's Man's Cry and God's Gracious Answer.
Frieze's Tenth and Twelfth Books of Quintilian.
Fullerton's (Lady G.) Too Strange Not to be True.
Funny Story Book.

Garland's Life of Randolph.
Gaskell's Life of Bronté. 2 vols.
The same, cheaper edition, in 1 vol.
George Ready.
Gerard's French Readings.
Gertrude's Philip Randolph.
Gesenius' Hebrew Grammar.
Ghostly Colloquies.

Gibbes' Documentary History. 3 vols.
Gibbons' Banks of New York.
Gilfillan's Literary Portraits.
Gillespie on Land Surveying.
Girardin on Dramatic Literature.
Goadby's Text-Book of Physiology.
Goethe's Iphigenia in Tauris.
Goldsmith's Essays.
——— Vicar of Wakefield.
Gosse's Evenings with the Microscope.
Goulburn's Office of the Holy Communion.
——— Idle Word.
——— Manual of Confirmation.
——— Sermons.
——— Study of the Holy Scriptures.
——— Thoughts on Personal Religion.
Gould's (E. S.) Comedy.
Gould's (W. M.) Zephyrs.
Graham's English Synonymes.
Grandmamma Easy's Toy Books.
Grandmother's Library. 6 vols. in case.
Grand's Spanish Arithmetic.
Grant's Report on the Armies of the United States 1864-'65.
Grauet's Portuguese Grammar.
Grayson's Theory of Christianity.
Greek Testament.
Greene's (F. H.) Primary Botany.
—— Class-Book of Botany.
Greene's (G. W.) Companion to Ollendorff.
—— First Lessons in French.
—— First Lessons in Italian.
—— Middle Ages.
Gregory's Mathematics.
Griffin on the Gospel.
Griffith's Poems.
Griswold's Republican Court.
——— Sacred Poets.
Guizot's (Madame) Tales.
Guizot's (M.) Civilization in Europe. 4 vols.
—— School edition. 1 vol.
—— New Edition, on tinted paper. 4 vols.
Gurowski's America and Europe.
——— Russia as it is.

Hadley's Greek Grammar.
Hahn's Greek Testament.
Hall's (B. H.) Eastern Vermont.
Hall's (C. H.) Notes on the Gospels. 2 vols.
Hall's (E. H.) Guide to the Great West.
Halleck's Poems.
—— Poems. Pocket size, blue and gold.
—— Young America.
Halleck's (H. W.) Military Science.
Hamilton's (Sir Wm.) Philosophy.
Hamilton's (A.) Writings. 6 vols.

Hand-Books on Education.
Hand-Book of Anglo-Saxon Root-Words.
Hand-Book of Anglo-Saxon Derivatives.
Hand-Book of the Engrafted Words.
Handy-Book of Property Law.
Happy Child's Library. 18 vols. in case.
Harkness' First Greek Book.
—— Latin Grammar.
—— First Latin Book.
—— Second "
—— Latin Reader.
Hase's History of the Church.
Haskell's Housekeeper's Encyclopædia.
Hassard's Life of Archbishop Hughes.
—— Wreath of Beauty.
Haupt on Bridge Construction.
Haven's Where There's a Will There's a Way.
—— Patient Waiting no Loss.
—— Nothing Venture Nothing Have.
—— Out of Debt Out of Danger.
—— Contentment Better than Wealth.
—— No Such Word as Fail.
—— All's Not Gold that Glitters.
—— A Place for Everything, and Everything in its Place.
—— Loss and Gain.
—— Pet Bird.
—— Home Series of Juvenile Books. 8 vols. in case.
Haven (Memoir of Alice B.).
Hazard on the Will.
Hecker's Questions of the Soul.
Hemans' Poems. 2 vols.
—— Songs of the Affections.
Henck's Field-Book for Engineers.
Henry on Human Progress.
Herbert's Poems.
Here and There.
Herodotus, by Johnson (in Greek).
Herodotus, by Rawlinson (in English). 4 vols.
Heydenreich's German Reader.
Hickok's Rational Cosmology.
—— Rational Psychology.
History of the Rebellion, Military and Naval. Illustrated.
Hoffman's Poems.
Holcombe's Leading Cases.
—— Law of Dr. and Cr.
—— Letters in Literature.
Holly's Country Seats.
Holmes' (M. A.) Tempest and Sunshine.
—— English Orphans.
Holmes' (A.) Parties and Principles.
Homes of American Authors.
Homer's Iliad.
Hooker's Complete Works. 2 vols.
Hoppin's Notes.
Horace, edited by Lincoln.
Howitt's Child's Verse-Book.
—— Juvenile Tales. 14 vols. in case.
How's Historical Shakspearian Reader.
—— Shakspearian Reader.
Huc's Tartary and China.
Hudson's Life and Adventures.
Humboldt's Letters.
Hunt's (C. H.) Life of Livingston.
Hunt's (F. W.) Historical Atlas.
Huntington's Lady Alice.
Hutton's Mathematics.
Huxley's Man's Place in Nature.
—— Origin of Species.

Iconographic Encyclopædia. 6 vols.—4 Text and 2 Plates.
Or, separately:
The Countries and Cities of the World. 2 vols.
The Navigation of all Ages. 2 vols.
The Art of Building in Ancient and Modern Times. 2 vols.
The Religions of Ancient and Modern Times. 2 vols.
The Fine Arts Illustrated. 2 vols.
Technology Illustrated. 2 vols.
Internal Revenue Law.
Iredell's Life. 2 vols.
Italian Comedies.

Jacobs' Learning to Spell.
—— The same, in two parts.
Jaeger's Class-Book of Zoology.
James' (J. A.) Young Man.
James' (H.) Logic of Creation.
James' (G. P. R.) Adrien.
Jameson's (Mrs.) Art Works.
—— Legends of Saints and Martyrs. 2 vols.
—— Legends of the Monastic Orders.
—— Legends of the Madonna.
—— History of Our Lord. 2 vols.
Jarvis' Reply to Milner.
Jay on American Agriculture.
Jeffers on Gunnery.
Jeffrey's (F.) Essays.
Johnson's Meaning of Words.
Johnson's (Samuel) Rasselas.
Johnston's Chemistry of Common Life. 2 vols.

Kavanagh's Adele.
—— Beatrice.
—— Daisy Burns.
—— Grace Lee.
—— Madeleine.
—— Nathalie.
—— Rachel Gray.
—— Seven Years.
—— Queen Mab.
—— Women of Christianity.
Keats' Poems.

Keep a Good Heart.
Keightley's Mythology.
Keil's Fairy Stories.
Keith (Memoir of Caroline P.)
Kendrick's Greek Ollendorff.
Kenny's Manual of Chess.
Kinglake's Crimean War. Vols. 1 and 2.
Kirke White's Poems.
Kirkland's Life of Washington.
A Cheaper Edition, for Schools.
Knowles' Orlean Lamar.
Kœppen's Middle Ages.
—— Separately—Middle Ages, 2 vols.
—— Atlas.
Kohlrausch's History of Germany.
Kuhner's Greek Grammar.

Lafever's Beauties of Architecture.
Lady Alice.
Lamartine's Confidential Disclosures.
—— History of Turkey. 3 vols.
Lancelott's Queens of England, and their Times. 2 vols.
Landon's (L. E.) Complete Works.
Latham's English Language.
Layard's Nineveh. Illustrated.
—— Cheap edition. Without Illustrations.
Learning to Spell.
Le Brun's Telemaque.
Lecky's Rise and Influence of Rationalism. 2 vols.
Le Sage's Adventures of Gil Blas. 1 vol.
—— Gil Blas, in Spanish.
Letter Writer.
Letters from Rome.
Lewes' (G. H.) History of Philosophy. 2 vols.
—— In 1 vol.
—— Physiology of Common Life.
Library of Travel and Adventure. 3 vols. in case.
Library for my Young Countrymen. 9 vols. in case.
Libro Primario de Ortografia.
Liebig's Laws of Husbandry.
Life of Man Symbolized by the Months of the Year.
Light and Darkness
Lights and Shadows of New York Picture Galleries.
Lindsay's Poems.
Linn's Life and Services.
Little Builder.
Little Engineer.
Livy, with English Notes.
Logan's Château Frissac.
Looking Glass for the Mind.
Lord's Poems.
—— Christ in Hades: a Poem.
Louise.
Lunt's Origin of the Late War.
Lyell's Elements of Geology.
Lyell's Principles of Geology.
Lyra Americana.
Lyra Anglicana.

Macaulay's Essays. 1 vol.
—— Essays. 7 vols.
—— Essays. A New and Revised Edition, on tinted paper. 6 vols.
Mackintosh's (Sir James) Essays.
Madge.
Mahan's Answer to Colenso.
—— Numerals of Scripture.
Mahon's England. 2 vols.
Maiu's Novum Testamentum Græce.
Mandeville's New Series of Readers.
1. Primary Reader.
2. Second Reader.
3. Third Reader.
4. Fourth Reader.
5. Fifth Reader.
Mandeville's Course of Reading.
—— Reading and Oratory.
—— First Spanish Reader.
—— Second Spanish Reader.
—— Third Spanish Reader.
Magnall's Historical Questions.
Man's Cry and God's Gracious Answer.
Manners' At Home and Abroad.
—— Sedgemoor.
Manning's Temporal Mission of the Holy Ghost.
—— The Reunion of Christendom.
Manual of Matrimony.
Markham's History of England.
Marrayat's Africa.
—— Masterman Ready.
—— Popular Novels. 12 vols.
—— A New and Revised Edition, printed on tinted paper 12 vols.
Marryat's Settlers in Canada.
Marshall's (E. C.) Book of Oratory.
—— First Book of Oratory.
Marshall's (T. W.) Notes on Episcopacy.
Marsh's Double Entry Book-keeping.
—— Single Entry Book-keeping.
—— Bank Book-keeping.
—— Book-keeping (in Spanish).
—— Blank Books for Double Entry. 6 books in set.
—— Do. for Single Entry. 6 books in set.
Martha's Hooks and Eyes.
Martineau's Crofton Boys.
—— Peasant and Prince.
Mary Lee.
Mary Staunton.
Mathews on Whist.
Mayhew's Illustrated Horse Docto
May's Bertram Noel.
—— Louis' School Days.
—— Mortimer's College Life.
—— Sunshine of Greystone.
McCormick's Visit to Sebastopol.

McIntosh's Aunt Kitty's Tales.
——— Charms and Counter Charms.
——— Evenings at Donaldson Manor.
——— Lofty and Lowly. 2 vols.
——— Maggie and Emma.
——— Meta Gray.
——— Two Lives.
——— Two Pictures.
——— New Juvenile Library. 7 vols. in case.
McLee's Alphabets.
McWhorter's Church Essays.
Meadows' Italian Dictionary.
Memoirs of Catharine II.
Merchant of Venice.
Merivale's History of the Romans. 7 vols.
Conversion of the Roman Empire.
" " Northern Nations.
Merry Christmas Book.
Michelet's France. 2 vols.
Milhouse's Italian Dictionary. 2 vols.
Mill's Political Economy. 2 vols.
Milledulcia.
Milton's Poems.
—— Paradise Lost.
Miniature Library. 27 vols.
Ministry of Life.
Minturn's Travels in India.
Modern British Essayists. 8 vols.
Modet's Light.
Moore's Revolutionary Ballads.
Moore's (George H.) Notes on the History of Slavery in Massachusetts.
Moore's (Thos.) Irish Melodies.
Moore's (Thos.) Memoirs and Journal. 2 vols.
—— Lallah Rookh.
—— Poems. 1 vol., cheap edition.
—— Do., on fine tinted paper.
Morales' Spanish Reader.
Moran on Money.
More's Practical Piety. 2 vols.
—— Private Devotions.
—— Domestic Tales.
—— Rural Tales.
—— Village Tales. 2 vols. in 1.
Morin's Practical Mechanics.
Morphy's Chess Games.
—— Triumphs.
Mulligan's English Grammar.
My Cave Life in Vicksburg.

Napoleon Bonaparte, by F. de l'Ardeche.
Napoleon Correspondence. 2 vols.
New Fairy Stories.
Newcomb on Financial Policy.
Newman's Apologia Pro Vita Sua.
——— Sermons.
New Testament, with engravings on wood from designs by the ancient masters. 1 vol.
New Testament, with Comment by E. Churton and W. B. Jones. 2 vols.
New York City Banks.
New York Picture Galleries.
Nightcap Series of Juveniles. 6 vols. in case.
Nightingale on Nursing.
Novum Testamentum, interpret. Beza.
Nueva Biblioteca de la Risa.
Nuovo Tesoro di Schergos.
Nursery Basket.

O'Callaghan's New Netherlands. 2 vols.
Œhlschlager's German Reader.
Ogilby on Lay Baptism.
Oldfellow's Uncle Nat.
Oliphant's Katmandu.
Ollendorff's English Grammar for Spaniards.
A Key to the Exercises.
—— English Grammar for Germans.
A Key to the Exercises.
—— French Grammar, by Jewett.
A Key to the Exercises.
—— French Grammar, by Value.
A Key to the Exercises.
—— French Grammar for Spaniards.
Key to the same.
—— German Grammar.
A Key to the Exercises.
—— Italian Grammar.
A Key to the Exercises.
—— Spanish Grammar.
A Key to the Exercises.
Ortografia.
Ordronaux' Hints on Health.
Oriental Library. 5 vols. in case.
Osgood's Hearthstone.
—— Mile Stones.
Ostervald's Nouveau Testament.
Otis' Landscapes. 1 vol.
—— The same, in 6 parts.
—— Studies of Animals. 1 vol.
—— Studies of Animals. 6 parts.
Overman's Metallurgy.
Owen's (Jno. J.) Acts of the Apostles.
—— Greek Reader.
—— Homer's Odyssey.
—— Homer's Iliad.
—— Thucydides.
—— Xenophon's Anabasis.
—— Xenophon's Cyropædia.
Owen's Penmanship. 3 books.

Paez' Geografia del Mundo.
Pages and Pictures. From the writings of James Fenimore Cooper.
Paine's Tent and Harem.
Palenzuela's Gramatica Inglesa.
Key to the same.
Palmer's Book-keeping.

Parker's Critical and Miscellaneous Writings.
—— Speeches and Addresses. 3 vols.
—— Additional Speeches. 2 vols.
—— Sermons of Theism.
—— Ten Sermons.
—— Trial and Defence.
—— Two Christmas Celebrations.
—— Works. 2 vols.
—— (Life of Theodore). 2 vols.
Parley's Faggots for the Fireside.
—— Present for all Seasons.
Parley's Wanderers by Sea and Land.
Patton's History of the United States.
Paul and Virginia.
Pearson on the Creed.
Perkins' Primary Arithmetic.
—— Elementary Arithmetic.
—— Practical Arithmetic.
—— The same, in Spanish.
—— A Key to Practical Arithmetic.
—— Higher Arithmetic.
—— Algebra.
—— Higher Algebra.
—— Geometry.
—— Higher Geometry.
—— Plane Trigonometry.
Perry's Americans in Japan.
—— Expedition to the China Seas and Japan.
Petit's Household Mysteries.
Peyrac's Comment on Parle à Paris.
Phelan on Billiards.
Phœnixiana.
Picture Gallery, in Spanish.
Pickell's Narrative. History of the Potomac Company.
Planches' Lead Diseases.
Plato's Apology.
Poetical Gems. Blue and Gold. 6 vols. in case.
Poets' Gallery.
Pollok's Poems.
Pomeroy's Municipal Law.
Pope's Poems.
Porter's Scottish Chiefs.
Portraits of my Married Friends.
Practical Cook Book.
Pratt's Dawnings of Genius.
Prince Charlie.
Pulpit Cyclopædia and Minister's Companion.
Punch's Pocket-Book of Fun.
Punchinello.
Pure Gold.
Pusey's Eirenicon.
Putz's Ancient Geography.
—— Mediæval Geography.
—— Modern Geography.

Quackenbos' First Book in English Grammar.
—— English Grammar.
—— First Lessons on Composition.
Quackenbos' Advanced Course of Composition and Rhetoric.
—— Natural Philosophy.
—— Primary History.
—— History of the United States.
—— Primary Arithmetic.
—— Elementary Arithmetic.
—— Practical Arithmetic.
Queens of England: a Series of Portraits.

Railway Anecdote Book.
Rawlinson's Herodotus. 4 vols.
Recreative Readings in French.
Reid's English Dictionary.
Reminiscences of a Zouave.
Replies to Essays and Reviews.
Republican Court.
Report on the Hygienic Condition of New York City.
Report of the United States Revenue Commission.
Reynard the Fox. After the version of Goethe.
Reynolds on Hand-Railings.
Rice's (Harvey) Poems.
Richards' At Home and Abroad.
—— Pleasure and Profit.
—— Harry's Vacation.
—— Electron.
Ricord's Youth's Grammar.
Ripalda's Spanish Catechism.
Robbins' Book of Poetry.
—— Guide to Knowledge.
Robertson's English Course for Spaniards, with Key.
Roemer's First French Reader.
—— Second French Reader.
—— Polyglot Readers—comprising English Text: French, German, Spanish, and Italian Translations.
Rosa Mystica.
Rosales' Caton Christiana.
Round the Block.
Rowan's French Reader.
—— French Revolution. 2 vols.
Royo's Instruccion Moral.

St. Pierre's Paul and Virginia.
Saintaine's Picciola. (In French.)
Sallust, with Notes.
Sampson's Brief Remarker.
Sandham's Twin Sisters.
Sanitary Condition of New York.
Sarmiento's Lectura Gradual.
Savarin's Hand-Book of Dining.
Schedel's Emancipation of Faith. 2 vols.
Schmidt's Ancient Geography.
Schmucker's History of the Four Georges.
Schwegler's History of Philosophy.
Scott's Lady of the Lake.
—— Lay of the Last Minstrel.

Scott's Marmion.
—— Poems, 16mo.
—— Poems, 8vo.
Scott's Soldier's Book.
Seoane and Neuman's Spanish Dictionary.
—— The same, abridged.
Sermons by the Paulists.
Sewell's Amy Herbert.
—— Cleve Hall.
—— Earl's Daughter.
—— Experience of Life.
—— Glimpse of the World.
—— Gertrude.
—— Ivors. 2 vols.
—— Katharine Ashton. 2 vols.
—— Laneton Parsonage. 3 vols.
—— Margaret Percival. 2 vols.
—— School Journal.
—— Ursula. 2 vols.
Sewell's Early Church.
—— Night Lessons.
—— Passing Thoughts.
—— Principles of Education.
—— History of Rome.
—— History of Greece.
Sewell's (R.) Bounty, Pension, and Prize Laws.
Shader's Copy-Books.
Shakspeare's Works. 1 thick vol., 8vo.
—— Works, 2 vols., 8vo.
—— Works, 1 vol., 8vo.
—— Works. 4 vols., 8vo.
Shakspeare Gallery.
—— Tempest. Illustrated.
Sherbrooke. By H. F. G. Author of "Madge."
Sherlock's Practical Christian.
Sigourney's Letters of Life.
Silber's Progressive Lessons in Greek.
Silver's Answer to Colenso.
—— Symbolic Character.
Simonne's French Grammar for Spaniards.
—— Key to the same.
—— French Verbs.
Sketches and Skeletons of Sermons.
Smith's (A.) Astronomy, in Spanish.
—— Geography, in Spanish.
Smith's (H.) Gaieties and Gravities.
Smith's (J.) Life.
Smith's (J.W.) Mercantile Law.
Smith's (P.) Universal History. 8 vols.
Smith's (S.) Works.
Smoker's Text-Book.
Southard on Godliness.
Southey's Oliver Cromwell.
—— Poems.
—— The same, cheap edition.
Southgate's Syrian Church.
Souvestre's Attic Philosopher.
—— Family Journal.
Soyer's Modern Cookery.
Spalding on English Literature.
Speckter's Picture Fables.

Spectator (The). 6 vols.
Spencer's Classification of the Sciences.
—— Education.
—— Essays: Moral, Political, and Æsthetic.
—— First Principles.
—— Illustrations of Progress.
—— Social Statics.
—— Works. 5 vols.
—— Psychology.
—— Biology. Vol. I.
Spenser's Poems.
Spiers' (Jewett) French and English Dictionary.
—— School French and English Dictionary.
Spiers' and Surenne's French Dictionary.
—— New Abridged Edition.
Spiritual Conceits. Extracted from the writings of the Fathers.
Sprague's History of the Florida War.
Stabat Mater.
Stearn's Shakspeare's Medical Knowledge.
Stratford Gallery.
Strickland's Queens of England: a Series of Portraits.
Story of a Genius.
Surenne's French Dictionary.
—— New French Manual.
Sutton's Learn to Live.
Swarts' Letters.
Swett on Consumption.

Tacitus' Histories, by Tyler.
—— Germania and Agricola.
Tales for the People.
Talfourds and Stephens' Essays.
Tappan's Elements of Logic.
—— Travels in Europe. 2 vols.
Tasso, by Wiffen.
Taylor (Jeremy) on Episcopacy.
—— Holy Living and Dying.
Taylor's (W. C.) Manual of History.
Separate: Ancient History.
Modern History.
Tegg's Chronology.
Templeton's Millwright's Companion.
Thackeray the Humourist and the Man of Letters.
—— Barry Lyndon. 2 vols.
—— Book of Snobs.
—— Mr. Brown's Letters.
—— Fitz-Boodle.
—— Jeames' Diary.
—— Men's Wives.
—— Paris Sketch-Book.
—— Punch's Novelist.
—— Shabby Genteel Story.
—— Yellowplush Papers.
—— Works. 6 vols.
—— Dr. Birch.
Thiers' French Revolution. 4 vols.
—— Cheap Edition. 2 vols.

Thomson's Seasons.
Thorpe's Bee-Hunter.
Thoughts in Affliction.
Tin Trumpet.
Tokens of Affection. 5 vols.
Tolon's Spanish Reader.
Towle's History of Henry the Fifth.
Treasury of Travel and Adventure.
Trench on the Miracles.
——— " Parables.
——— " " Condensed.
Trescott's Diplomacy.
Truran on Iron Manufacture.
Tyndall on Heat and Motion.
——— On Radiation.
Tyng's Four Gospels.

Uhlemann's Syriac Grammar.
Uncle John's Library. 6 vols. in case.
Upfold's Manual of Devotions.
Ure's Dictionary, with Supplement, 3 vols.
—— Supplement separately.

Vandenhoff's Note Book.
Vaughan's Revolutions of Race.
Velazquez' Spanish Dictionary.
——— Abridged.
——— Spanish Conversations.
——— Spanish Reader.
Vignettes (Cooper's), from Drawings by F. O. C. Darley.
Villas on the Hudson.
Virgil's Æneid.
Virginia Comedians. 2 vols.
Voltaire's Charles XII., in French.

Wainwright's Sermons.
Walworth's Gentle Skeptic.
Ward's Lyrical Recreations.
Ward's Naval Tactics.
Warner's (A. B.) My Brother's Keeper.
Warner's (Miss) Hills of the Shatemuc.
Warner's (J. F.) Lessons in Music.
Watson's Men and Times.
Watt's (James) Life.
Waverley Gallery.
Webster's Spelling Book. New Edition
Webster's Quarto Dictionary, Unabridged.
——— Primary Dictionary.
——— Common School Dictionary.
——— High School Dictionary.
——— Academic Dictionary.
——— Counting-House and Family Dictionary.
——— Pocket Dictionary.
Week's Delight.
Welby's Poems.
Wells' Things Not Generally Known.
Wentz's Smiles and Frowns.
Whewell's Inductive Sciences. 2 vols.
Whist, by Cœlebs.
White's (Rev. J.) Eighteen Christian Centuries.
White's (Rev. J.) History of France.
White's (R. G.) Shakspeare's Scholar.
White's (Kirke) Poems.
Whitehead's History of Perth Amboy.
——— New Jersey.
Whitney's Poems.
Whiton's First Lessons in Greek.
Wife's Stratagem.
Wight's Translation of Cousin.
——— Edition of Hamilton.
Williams' Isthmus of Tehuantepec. 2 vols.
Wilmott's Summer Journal.
Wilson's Sacra Privata.
Wilson's (Prof. John) Essays.
Wilson's (J.) Price Book.
Wilson's (Rev. W. D.) Treatise on Logic.
Winkleman's French Syntax.
Winslow's Moral Philosophy.
Winter Evening Library. 8 vols. in case.
Woman's Worth.
Wood's Marrying Too Late.
Wood (J. G.) Homes without Hands.
World-Noted Women.
Worthen's Rudimentary Drawing.
——— First Lessons in Mechanics.
Wright's (A. D.) Primary Lessons.
Wright's (J. H.) Ocean Work.
Wyatt's Christian Altar.

Xenophon's Anabasis, by Boise.
——— Memorabilia, by Robbins.

Yonge's Beechcroft.
—— Ben Sylvester's Word.
—— Castle Builders.
—— Clever Woman of the Family.
—— Daisy Chain. 2 vols.
—— The Trial.
—— Dynevor Terrace. 2 vols.
—— Friarswood Post Office.
—— Heartsease. 2 vols.
—— Heir of Redclyffe. 2 vols.
—— Hopes and Fears.
—— Kenneth.
—— Lances of Lynwood.
—— Richard the Fearless.
—— Stokesley Secret.
—— Two Guardians.
—— Young Stepmother. 2 vols.
—— The Dove in the Eagle's Nest.
Young American's Library. 9 vols. in case.
Youmans' Alcohol and Man.
——— Class-Book of Chemistry.
——— Chart of Chemistry, on roller.
——— Chemical Atlas.
——— Household Science.
Young's Poems.
Youth's Book of Nature.

Zschokke's Goldmaker's Village.

www.ingramcontent.com/pod-product-compliance
Lightning Source LLC
LaVergne TN
LVHW020225110826
845151LV00003B/828

* 9 7 8 1 4 2 5 5 3 1 5 2 2 *